Illustrated by El Davo

To Wilbur,
Thanks for spreading happiness
everywhere you go.
You brighten up life.
Dad
x

Praise for Todd's original book, *Own Life*

Dan Richards
The Best Book I have Ever Set Eyes On
I've just got to Chapter 3 and I can officially say (with tears in my eyes, that's how good it is!) that this is the best book I have ever set eyes on. That is because it's not just another self-help book, it's more like an EXAM of your life, LITERALLY.

It's mind blowing! and I have also not stopped writing, as he states to 'pick up your pen and write' and I've never felt so indulged to do so, because he wants to you really go in depth and explore your life and what he is asking of you.
I have found it simply INCREDIBLE, that I couldn't help but do an early review which I never normally tend to do but I have been mind-blown by this book, and I feel by the end of it (as just by flicking through, you can see lots of 'reflect and write' scattered throughout the book) I could become a completely different person! this is what is so mesmerising.

R. Bajic
Want to Know Yourself?
A very easy read and takes what most people consider the difficult parts of their lives or confusing parts and breaks it down to understand yourself. There is no right or wrong in your life in this book. Just tries to lay it out so you can better understand yourself and what you want in life, what you want to achieve or just self-understanding of who you are. But in doing so you sort of get to understand others in your life too and how they are. The illustrations are brilliant too and help resonate the points the book is explaining.

David Robertson
This book is so good that I want to keep putting it down. Todd Eden has succeeded in creating a book on personal development that is genuinely and profoundly thought-provoking. Right from the start, the questions, and exercises grabbed my attention and had me putting the book down to think and reflect. I have always a very occasional journaler, but since reading Own Life I have been loving finding quiet moments throughout the day to focus on the bigger questions. The book is both practical and energising. It helps you to reflect on what really matters to you, but then it helps you to put in place practical and actionable strategies to help you take control of your life. I love it.

Todd has taught thousands of delegates around the world, and after completing the course, each one is asked, 'What will you do differently now?'

Here follows a selection of their responses, which all start with

"I will…"

'… achieve my goals whatever it may take.' [Charidimos V]
'… be much more confident.' [Hadra A]
'… be more confident talking to new people.' [Elizabeth G]
'… be more grateful about being myself.' [Mohamad A]
'… be a better version of myself.' [Nicole E]
'… believe in myself.' [Maddi M]
'… change.' [Alex M]
'… achieve my potential.' [Abdulla R]
'… be more productive.' [Fahmid C]
'… feel comfortable being myself to others.' [Elissar B]
'… be more resilient to the voices in my head.' [Natasha J]
'… be more aware of the potential that I have.' [Emine O]
'… start improving my habits and focus on priorities.' [Marta M]
'… be more interactive with others.' [Dongho L]
'… manage my problems well.' [Umar T]
'… be more open.' [Marta O]
'… handle setbacks better.' [Rosemary C]
'… stop coming up with excuses.' [Javor G]
'… be more positive.' [Mathilda C]
'… be more motivated to achieve my goals.' [Iva K]
'… strive to better my self-discipline.' [Sean M]
'… step out of my comfort zone.' [Margherita C]
'… be more organized.' [Abdul R]
'… have more purpose in everything I do.' [Luksa K]

'... be more committed towards my goals.' [Mohamed A]

'... be more productive.' [Sharon S]

'... face my fears.' [Tanu C]

'... be more confident in myself.' [Madalina M]

'... have purpose in my actions.' [Louise M]

'... face the tasks that I avoid because of fear.' [James W]

'... step out of my comfort zone.' [Daniela B]

'... start changing unhealthy habits.' [Augustin L]

'... set goals for myself.' [Nilay S]

'... pursue my goals.' [Jeremiah U]

'... implement mindfulness.' [Lauren C]

'... be an active listener.' [Anira B]

'... set my goals.' [Imani S]

'... know myself better.' [Abhishek B]

'... not be afraid to share my thoughts with others.' [Disha S]

'... make the most of what I have.' [Tiffany D]

'... be more authentic.' [Ellarene C]

'... accept myself.' [Alice V]

'... apply for jobs I was unsure about.' [Marco A]

'... believe in my ability.' [Hannah S]

'... be more confident in myself.' [Amy F]

'... appreciate different opinions.' [Ana M]

'... work harder towards my goals.' [Andres G]

'... face my future strong.' [Arjunan R]

'... commit with purpose.' [Camilo R]

'... push myself to leave my comfort zone.' [Daniel C]

'... keep improving myself.' [Emmanuel O]

'... control my inner voice.' [Hiren T]

'... be a better leader.' [Ieva G]

'... adopt mindfulness and talk to strangers.' [James T]

'... feel more confident around people.' [Jessica F]

'... be more self-aware.' [Kabilas P]

'... feel more confident to apply for certain jobs.' [Katherine H]

'... put myself in the shoes of others more often.' [Kilian B]

'... take responsibility for my life.' [Lanja R]

'... take risks.' [Lauren M]

'... get out of my comfort zone.' [Madhumitha K]

'... listen more.' [Michal C]

'... be more confident.' [Nantia B]

'... have more confidence in myself.' [Polly S]

'... be more mindful.' [Rosie G]

'... be more ready to take the lead.' [Samuel S]

'... be more introspective.' [Sian W]

'... take better care of my health.' [Sushma S]

'... always say positive things about myself.' [Toyyibat B]

'... be more resilient.' [Yakubu S]

'... be willing to step out of my comfort zone.' [Sabrina C]

'... continue to be me.' [Samantha C]

'... make a difference.' [Debbie F]

'... believe in myself more.' [Manvinder D]

'... express myself better.' [Hasit G]

'... be kinder to myself.' [Jad J]

'... trust other people more.' [Ashley A]

'... stop trying to solve other people's problems.' [Brandon M]

'... be more understanding.' [Noi B]

By the end of this book, what will you be doing?

CONTENTS

HOW TO GROW INTO THE BEST VERSION OF YOURSELF

I'm standing backstage. I feel a bead of sweat roll down my armpit, soaking into my best shirt, and hope the growing damp patch isn't obvious through the V-necked sweater I'm also wearing. The speaker before me finishes, the audience is quiet. No applause. He turns, walks towards me and pushes the microphone into my wet trembling hands. Ten paces to the front of the stage. 150 people standing in small cliques taking bites from buffet food. I stand, looking into individual pairs of eyes. Slowly the room becomes more quiet, more still, until you could hear a pin drop. Will my voice come out at all, I wonder.

'Raise your hand if you would like greater self-confidence,' my first line arrives surprisingly clearly.

I count to three. Then a hand goes up, followed by another. Reassured that it's OK to show vulnerability, one by one, every person in the room raises their hand.

Into the stillness I ask, 'If you had greater self-confidence, what would you do?' Pause. 'Turn to the person next to you and share what you see this more confident version of yourself achieving.'

That's it. The noise rises and rises. Animated conversations are springing up everywhere. Virtual strangers opening up to one another.

See, you and I are not alone. We'd both like a little more self-confidence, and so would everyone else. And if we could have it, we'd use it to Own Life more fully. Henry Ford once said, 'If you believe you can, or believe you can't. You are right.'

This book will help you become more connected with the person you are today, leading to a greater acceptance for who you are right now. Then, with a growth mindset, we'll imagine the emergence of a best version of you.

Together, let's find that more confident 'you' and see what magic you're capable of.

HOW TO OWN LIFE

This may not be your first book from the Own Life Collection so you'll recognise this guidance, and if you're new to the series, then welcome! ;-).

To truly Own Life takes some time, so be patient with the book and yourself. Give the concepts space to breathe, and your experiments the necessary time to achieve their desired results. In every book in the collection, you'll be learning how to live with greater self-confidence and how to set your path to own your future.

Unlike many self-help books, we are not attempting to turn you into someone new, to add another mask, which is exhausting to live up to. You will always be you, and we want you to be ALL of you, ALL of the time.

When you allow yourself, being you is so easy, and nobody else does it better!

This is your life journey, and this is your book. At the moment the book in your hand looks like anybody else's, but shortly you'll start to add your own notes, in your own way, with your unique handwriting, and instantly this book is like no other on the planet.

Your life is also in your hands. How much you own it depends on how much you invest in it. In a moment you'll be answering a set of questions which will put you on the path to becoming more self-aware, and it's through the lens of 'yourself' that we'll do great work together. Yes, there are models and theories, lots of them in fact, but it's how you relate to them that matters – so when there's a pause in the text and a question for you to ponder, really do it.

Throughout the book, you'll see sections titled 'Reflect & Write'. This is your invitation to do just that. Take some quiet time to consider each of the questions, allow your thoughts and feelings to emerge, and then crystalize them by putting pen to paper. The act of writing down your thoughts helps them to settle in your mind and brings a comforting level of clarity. I don't think of you as readers, I think of you as participants, so read this book with a pen in your hand.

The insights you gain about yourself can be revelatory yet remain merely interesting. To shift the dial of your life requires action, and throughout the book you'll be invited to conduct small experiments to tweak your ingrained behaviours.

From time to time, you may have a question that you need some help with; or maybe you'd like to connect with others who are struggling with similar issues; or would like to share a moment of enlightenment, or a piece of advice; or be inspired by other people's Own Life journey. For any of this, head to www.ownlife.me/connect and we'll take this journey together.

HOW'S IT ALL GOING?

Before we start, it's helpful to get a baseline on how things are really going for you. We're starting with a wide lens to check in on how fully you are Owning Life as a whole. We do this to put *OWN LIFE WITH CONFIDENCE* into context and to notice which other facets of life you might be able to draw strengths from, or which need additional support so they don't trip you up.

Put a date on the page, and if you've completed this task in previous books in the Own Life collection, do this again first before reading your notes from last time.

Reflect & Write: You've lived on this planet for quite some time now. How's it going? How is life turning out for you? On this occasion you'll notice that I give you a relatively small box to write in. We just want to get an overall impression at this stage.

Perhaps you're thinking, 'It's a huge freakin' mess, and I don't know how to dig myself out.' Or maybe, 'Things are actually going pretty well, but is this it?' No matter how you respond to this question, if you want to get the most out of life, then this book will help you discover the authentic human you are and lay the foundations for living the life you are truly capable of living.

Consider the statements below with real honesty based on your experience of the last six months. Decide to what extent you agree or disagree with each of them, and colour in the corresponding box in the chart on the next page.

1. I know and accept myself for who I am
2. I believe I can become good at anything I choose to put my mind to
3. I maintain a positive emotional state of mind regardless of what is going on around me
4. I push through fear to accomplish things that are uncomfortable
5. What I do is aligned to a deeply held sense of purpose
6. I make the most of life by using my time wisely
7. I am like a battery, always full of energy and ready to go
8. I enjoy trusting, respectful relationships with everyone in my life

	STRONGLY DISAGREE	DISAGREE	NEUTRAL	AGREE	STRONGLY AGREE
1.	☐	☐	☐	☐	☐
2.	☐	☐	☐	☐	☐
3.	☐	☐	☐	☐	☐
4.	☐	☐	☐	☐	☐
5.	☐	☐	☐	☐	☐
6.	☐	☐	☐	☐	☐
7.	☐	☐	☐	☐	☐
8.	☐	☐	☐	☐	☐

Even though it's good to know your start point, there's no need to judge it. Just imagine if you could nudge your scores further to the right? And just imagine what life would be like if you could live it way over to the right-hand column most of the time. That's our goal together.

Wherever you'd like to develop, there's a book in the Own Life collection for you. By fully participating in this book (*OWN LIFE WITH CONFIDENCE*) you will work on accepting yourself for who you are and develop into the person you would like to be.

In the future, if you want to foster great relationships then *OWN LIFE WITH TRUST* is the book for you. Or pick up *OWN LIFE WITH COURAGE* to learn how to manage your emotions and push through fear. And if you would like to engineer a lifestyle that fulfils your dreams, then *OWN LIFE*

WITH PURPOSE is the next book to add to your collection. Now you have your baseline, are you ready to live a more rewarding life? Sure you are. Let's jump into *OWN LIFE WITH CONFIDENCE.*

PART 1

WHO AM I?

CHAPTER 1
HOW CONFIDENT AM I?

Self-confidence is a feeling of trust in your abilities, qualities and judgement. Do you trust yourself?

If you do, then you believe you can achieve your goals and you'll find evidence you're right and the fortitude to persevere. If you don't trust yourself, you'll find evidence to back up your limiting self-judgement and step back from challenges.

Reflect & Write: How confident a person are you? (Notice the box is relatively large, try to fill it with your thoughts).

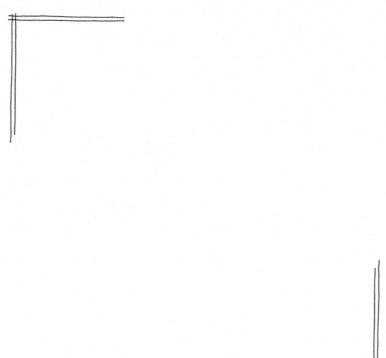

Did you say to yourself 'it depends on the circumstances'?

Of course, it does. So, scoring 'you' as a whole person isn't very helpful. With some people, you feel completely at ease. With other people, their mere presence is unsettling, and you begin to doubt yourself. Confidence depends on who is in the room with you. There are also likely to be occasions when you feel very confident, for example when you do something routine at work, and occasions when you feel less confident, perhaps when you're doing something for the first time.

It's easy to notice the low confidence moments because the body can set off all the fight or flight symptoms – a racing pulse, scrambled thoughts, sweaty palms, shallow breathing, light-headedness.

Reflect & Write: Acknowledge ten situations that cause you to feel low confidence.

This may have been an easy task for you to complete. Your low confidence moments may come with 'full-on' body experiences, and each moment may be pre-lived with anxiety before the event, and then re-lived over and over afterwards. The amount of time your mind spends in these situations is likely to be much longer than the actual situation itself.

Reflect & Write: OK. Let's go searching for the opposite scenario. Can you find ten moments when you felt high in confidence?

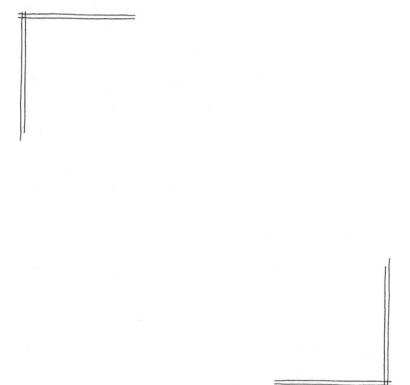

Is that more difficult to pin down? It's because we don't notice these moments; there are no amplified physical symptoms to bring these moments into our conscious awareness. Most of the time we just get on with something because we've learnt how to do it well, and we're on autopilot. While we're doing these things, our minds might actually be living in the negative fantasy world of a forthcoming low-confidence moment.

When I feel competent at what I'm doing, my mind wanders – I don't focus on how good I am at doing what I am doing. I make awesome pizzas from scratch and simply love the whole process from dough-making to serving up. I've made them so often that I can do it without thinking. I don't dance around the kitchen high-fiving and singing 'everything is awesome', I just quietly and happily get on with it. I'm a confident pizza maker, but I hadn't thought of it like this until just now.

Spend a little more time with the list of high confidence moments and see if you can add a few more. You're not necessarily looking for a physical 'high', simply things that come easy and take no mental or emotional energy. We don't spend any time thinking about these things and therefore haven't yet acquired the skill of noticing them. So be kind to yourself if your list seems short and if each point seems a little insignificant. Then be pleased you noticed them at all.

What would happen if you only ever faced situations you felt confident in?

You're likely to repeat things you've been doing over and over. And you'd never meet new people. You've already experienced everything you ever will. Your future looks the same as your past.

This may be fine for some people. But not for you. You want more. You want to own life.

Let's reframe things a little.

Those low confidence moments you listed are not defined by your level of confidence. They are retitled as – 'the things I am yet to master'. As your skill level develops, quite naturally, so does your confidence. There's no dark magic at play here. To build self-confidence is simply to build your capability to face situations you're likely to face in life.

Read this next line: 'I'm not a confident person.' That's the last time that you're going to say this to yourself. I'm not asking you to blindly lie to yourself and now say, 'I'm a supremely confident person.' I'm asking you to take the whole person (you) out of the judgement, and phrase it with a growth mindset by saying, 'There are situations I face when I feel lower in confidence because I haven't mastered them yet.' These situations may be chained together back-to-back to give the illusion they're one big thing: 'life' – that you haven't yet mastered. But life is made up of hundreds of smaller situations.

Which leads us nicely to two questions. What situations in life would you like to master, and how?

Reflect & Write: Imagine it is possible. Imagine you really could master some of those important situations that make up your life. Which ones would they be? Pick a couple. What impact would this have on your life?

Journey to Mastery

There are four stages to developing competence, and everything you have just listed sits in the lower-left quadrant of the chart below.

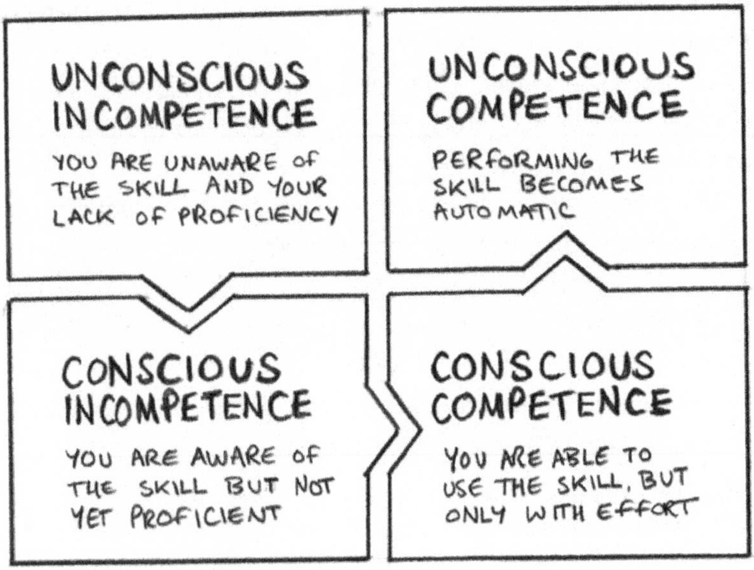

UNCONSCIOUS INCOMPETENCE

YOU ARE UNAWARE OF THE SKILL AND YOUR LACK OF PROFICIENCY

UNCONSCIOUS COMPETENCE

PERFORMING THE SKILL BECOMES AUTOMATIC

CONSCIOUS INCOMPETENCE

YOU ARE AWARE OF THE SKILL BUT NOT YET PROFICIENT

CONSCIOUS COMPETENCE

YOU ARE ABLE TO USE THE SKILL, BUT ONLY WITH EFFORT

You are aware that you lack the skill. When I first sat in the driving seat of a car as a teenager I was aware that I did not know how to drive. Yet I could see people around me every day making it look effortless.

This is actually the second stage in the competency model. The first stage (top left of the chart) is where you are blissfully unaware there is even a skill that is required. For example, before I started writing books I had no idea that it takes skill to craft an index (I was unconscious of my incompetence). As soon as I realised it was a skill I became consciously incompetent and knew it would be better for me to employ a professional to do the job.

Whatever skill you have ultimately mastered, you were once on the left-hand side of the chart. Then you took lessons, or received guidance, or learnt from failure. And slowly you were able to use the skill, but only with real concentration. For example, my instructor broke down the complex task of driving into lots of mini-steps, sometimes with phrases like 'mirror-signal-manoeuvre' to help me remember the sequence of things. At this point I had moved to the bottom right quadrant where I could successfully drive a car but only if I applied all my brain power – I was competent when applying consciousness.

With hours and hours of practice over the years, I now don't even notice I'm driving – it just seems to happen automatically. I've arrived at the final stage of the competence model where I am competent at the skill without even thinking about it. I'm competent without applying consciousness.

The first step to mastery and therefore greater confidence is to become just slightly more skilful at dealing with a situation. Then just slightly more skilful, and on and on. There's already something you can do better than anyone else on the planet... being you! And since being you happens unconsciously, it's sometimes difficult to really know who you are. Yet from this 'not-knowing' space you still judge yourself harshly. The first step on this journey therefore is to really get to know yourself. Then over the course of the book you will develop the skill of being you more fully.

CHAPTER 2
SOCIAL CONDITIONING

Who am I, and why am I here? These are two significant questions with which to begin a self-development journey. Since the answers are constantly evolving, you may never find THE answer to either. However, not to contemplate these fundamental questions is to hand over the steering wheel of life to others.

By the end of this section, you will have a strong sense of your own identity and be completely OK with who you are right now. We will achieve his by exploring how your upbringing has shaped your character. What sets you apart from everyone else – how are you unique? What do you have to offer the world, and what would you like your contribution to be?

Programming Children

The environment into which each of us is born is unique – different to everyone else on the planet through climate, history, culture, family shape, or sibling sequence. As babies, if our clan rejects us, we die, and therefore we are hard-wired with a longing for acceptance. To do this, we mimic others – taking particular notice of the behaviours of the grown-ups around us and conforming to fit in.

Even before we can talk, we begin to believe and value the same things as our society. These beliefs and values go in 'unfiltered', we're not judging at this age, we're absorbing. Children are likely to have the same beliefs about religion as their parents and in future, vote the same way. We learn what our parents determine to be useful or interesting, so our early skillset is programmed by the people around us.

All this comes together to shape our sense of identity; the things we say about ourselves (to ourselves). It's a list of 'I ams'. This whole process, whereby the significant people around us shape who we are, is termed 'social conditioning'.

You will see a little later how significant the impact of your specific social conditioning is on your daily habits, and to what extent you've already broken away from the

conditioning of your early years. Consciously choosing your own path is known as 'self-determination' and could also be the subtitle of the Own Life books.

How Your Brain Is Wired

Compared to every other species, human brains are born 'underdeveloped'. But it is this unfinished nature of the brain that is also our most significant strength – because it makes us adaptable. The human brain is shaped by the details of life experiences, so it's 'livewired' rather than 'hardwired'.[1]

It's not the number of brain cells that change (children and adults have the same amount), it's the way they're connected. Over the first two years of life, as we experience sensory information, the neurons become rapidly connected until we have over 100 trillion synapses. From this moment onwards, the unused connections are pared back until only half remain, while those we use most become stronger.

Imagine rain falling on a hillside. Individual drops evaporate and leave no trace, while others fall together, forming rivulets, and eventually have the power to cut deeply into the landscape. Every hill is unique, and every shower is different. So too is the physical structure of your brain, every single life experience has shaped its microscopic details. The way your brain is wired is shaped by your past and is therefore different to everyone else's on the planet.

Your Social Conditioning

If you were writing your autobiography and the first chapter was titled 'Age 0 to 13', what would you write about? You might mention your environment (including the people), the behaviours you were taught (deliberately and by observation), which skills were nurtured and the set of beliefs you adopted.

Reflect & Write: Write a few paragraphs to describe your life from birth to 13 years old.

Reflect & Write: Next, recall what it was like to be 13 years of age. Stand in your school shoes as though you have time travelled into the past and write a list of at least ten 'I am...' statements. For example, I am shy, I am easy-going and so on.

Let's now also capture the characters who shared the stage with you as you were growing up.

Reflect & Write: Think of the five people you spent most time with, who were they and what were they like? Write a short paragraph for each person.

Your upbringing has shaped you. So what shape are you now? In the next section, we'll find out.

Who are you today?

Leaving the memories of your teenage years behind, we'll jump to the present day and take a look at the person who is holding this book and reading this sentence.

What others see in you isn't you. It's a combination of what you're projecting (perhaps unconsciously), and what they notice (which depends on them, not you). So let's use this to your advantage and get some different perspectives.

Reflect & Write: Consider five people from different parts of your life who know you really well. If you asked each of them in turn, and in strict confidence, to describe you in five words, what would they say?

Step back from the 25 individual words you have just written and create a distance from the specific individuals whose shoes you have just been standing in. Are there some patterns or themes that emerge? Or perhaps you're a chameleon and are able to present yourself in different ways depending on the audience.

Reflect & Write: What is the image you are projecting into the world? Write about yourself as though you are describing a character in a movie. Start it with He/She...

CHAPTER 3
HOW VALUES SHAPE YOUR LIFE

What others say about you is based on the behaviours they experience from you. Unseen to them are the values which influence the way you behave. What you do is influenced by how you think. You hold intentions (which may be conscious or unconscious) which sit upon the bedrock of your values and shape your destiny.

Perhaps you've never considered what you value most and why – but you can deepen your self-awareness right now. Read through and annotate the following list of values. Tick ones that feel important to you, cross out the ones that are less important. Next, select up to seven that are the most important to you (at this moment in your life) and put a heavy ring around them so they stand out.

Accountability	Ethics	Job security
Achievement	Excellence	Justice
Adventure	Fairness	Kindness
Altruism	Faith	Knowledge
Ambition	Family	Leadership
Authenticity	Financial stability	Learning
Balance	Forgiveness	Legacy
Beauty	Freedom	Leisure
Being the best	Friendship	Love
Belonging	Fun	Loyalty
Career	Generosity	Making a
Caring	Giving back	difference
Collaboration	Grattitude	Nature
Commitment	Growth	Openness
Community	Harmony	Optimism
Compassion	Health	Order
Competence	Home	Parenting
Confidence	Honesty	Patience
Contribution	Hope	Patriotism
Courage	Humility	Peace
Curiousity	Humor	Perseverance
Dignity	Inclusion	Power
Diversity	Independence	Pride
Environment	Initiative	Recognition
Efficiency	Integrity	Reliability
Equality	Intuition	Respect

Reflect & Write: Write a sentence or two about each of the words you have circled. Why is it important to you?

Reflect & Write: Next, consider how each important value influences your behaviour. "Because I value _____, I ....' (For example, because I value order, I always tidy up everything and have a schedule I stick to; and can show irritation at others who don't do the same).

Before we go on to look at how you can live your values more fully, let's have a go at looking where they come from. Your circled words will be different to mine, in fact, there is a good chance that no-one else has circled the exact same words as you did. Your unique upbringing has shaped you, and therefore you too are unique. Have a go at explaining why you value these few things so deeply. First, look back at the list of five people you spent most time with when you were growing up. Have they shaped what you value most? Next, reflect on crossroad moments in your life – what events have had a lasting effect on the way you think?

Reflect & Write: From where did I pick up my most important values?

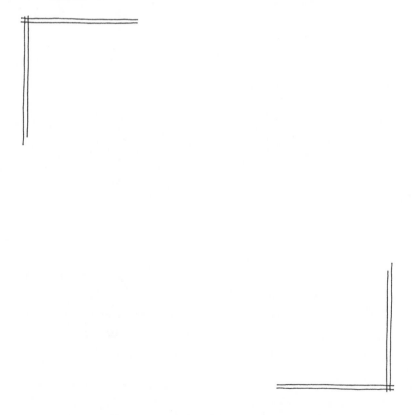

Now you're getting a good idea of who or what shaped the person you've become, let's use these positive values to further develop the skill of being you.

Reflect & Write: Score each of your circled values 0–10 based on how fully you have lived it over the past two weeks with 0 meaning not all and 10 meaning totally. (Imagine you'd been followed around with a video camera every waking moment for the last couple of weeks and others get to rate your performance on YouTube. What would be your average score?)

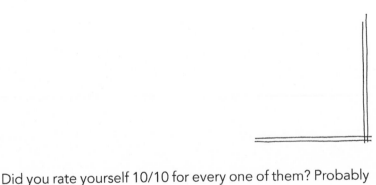

Did you rate yourself 10/10 for every one of them? Probably not. There's a range – some high, some low. Be OK with whatever the number is, this is self-awareness, not self-judgement.

Reflect & Write: Take one of the lower scores. Let's suspend judgement for a moment. If, with 'a click of the fingers' you are now living that value 10 out of 10 for the next month (without worrying about how this might happen), write down what is different for you, and what is different for others

You've now contemplated a more satisfying future where you are fully living this value, and you know your present reality (your score from the past two weeks). It's time to begin the development journey with a single small step.

Reflect & Write: What can you do in the next 48 hours to begin to shift your current score upwards? You're not looking for a giant leap (although it's OK if that's what happens), you're merely attempting to become unstuck – to shift a habit and begin to move in the right direction. If you wish, you can now decide what to do with each of the other four values – what small step would you like to take to begin living each value more fully by the end of the week?

Whilst we've got our headspace in 'values' let's journey to the future and begin to imagine what the 'best version' of you could be like.

We'll bank the circled list of values, you'll do the small steps to begin living them more fully, so let's imagine this trajectory continues so that over time you are 'unconsciously competent' at them all of the time (and maybe you are already). Now it's 'free pick' time. Go back to the original list of values – which contain your ticks and crossings out. Imagine the best version of you that could exist – which three values from the big list would you be living 10/10 every day?

Now remember, it's a free pick. You don't have to have ticked it earlier. You don't even have to be any good at it presently. For now, your only challenge is how to be a ruthless decision maker and reject a long list of values that would also be awesome to have.

Reflect & Write: What three values do I want to be living more fully in the future?

Now you know the value that's important for you to nurture. How does this translate into your future behaviours? Behaviours are the things you do. It's the things that others would be able to see you doing. It's the things that make a difference in life. For example, I might have selected 'family'. Now how would I translate this desire to live this value more fully, into actually being a guy whose life is more family orientated? There's lots of options I have, so let's get a few of them down on paper.

I could... call my parents more frequently, do MUCH better with my Mother's and Father's Day gifts, send them photos of their grandchildren each week. I could... stop writing this sentence and go and see my own kids who have just returned from school. I could... sit in my daughter's room for half an hour each evening for a chat, be the one to read to my son every night, plan a weekend getaway for my wife. I could do lots of things!

Over to you. Take each of the values you want to live more fully and fill the box with ideas on how you could (you're not committing to actually doing any of them – you're just collecting options).

Reflect & Write: How could you live these three free-pick values more fully (...in theory)?

Now just pick one behaviour for each value. And don't feel under any pressure to begin doing it now, or this week, or even this year. For now we're just getting a sense of what this future 'best version' of you is doing.

Collecting the full set of ten values you've been working with (the seven you circled and the three free picks), and using just ten succinct sentences, list the specific behaviours the future best version of you exhibits unconsciously.

Here's my list of ten:
Authenticity: I show up in all situations being the real Todd
Courage: I notice when fear is holding me back from something – I don't allow it to
Excellence: I set high standards for everything I do
Humour: I spread smiles in every interaction
Trust: I always do what I say I will do
Compassion: I stand in the shoes of others to connect with how they are feeling
Independence: I do what I feel is right even when opinions differ
Gratitude: I say thank you repeatedly during the day, and mean it each time
Kindness: I seek ways to be kind when there's no expectation of it
Serenity: I am able to empty my mind of thoughts and simply be present

Interestingly, as I was typing my list I was thinking what a cool person it would be who displayed all these things, all of the time. And I'm OK with me not being that person, or anywhere near it... yet. There are some behaviours on my list that come naturally (e.g. excellence), some that I work on (e.g. compassion), and some I definitely feel incompetent at (e.g. serenity).

So no judgement is required. I'm not doing a gap analysis between this mythical person I've just defined and the less perfect version of me that's here today. Remember, we're simply imagining the future best version of you.

Reflect & Write: For each of your ten values, write a sentence about the behaviour of your future best version.

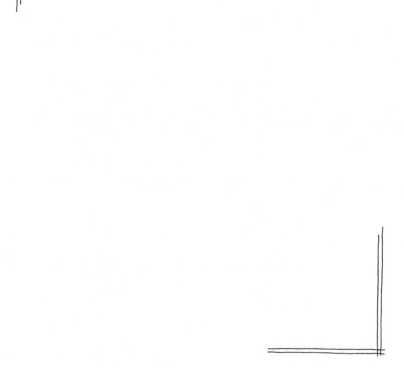

Your list is different to mine, right? We may have some values in common, but not all ten. And we definitely haven't chosen the precise words to describe our behaviours in the same way. This is what makes humans so wonderfully intriguing. We have different pictures in our minds about what a 'best version' looks like. I can read your version, and appreciate it, and think it's great. Yet it differs from the version I wrote down.

As you're building confidence remember this important point – you get to define the you that you want to be, and only you get to measure yourself against it.

Don't try to live up to someone else's image of the better version of you – not from a parent, a friend, a self-help book, a celebrity, a boss, a teacher, a partner, or social media. Have you been judging yourself against other people's expectations of what a good human looks like? It's one of the prime causes of low self-confidence.

Albert Einstein is often credited with the following quote: 'Everyone is a genius. But if you judge a fish by its ability to climb a tree, it will live its whole life believing that it is stupid.'

You are a genius at being you. Allow yourself the permission to be fully yourself.

That will do for now. Take a break before moving onto the next chapter where we investigate the beliefs you hold.

CHAPTER 4
THE BELIEFS YOU HOLD

Is the earth round or flat? Depending on when in history you grew up your answer would be different. A flat earth was a belief, which was once thought of as a truth. In life it's convenient for us to think of things as being fixed as it brings a reassuring stability in how we live it. But this causes us to assume things are facts rather than beliefs. Lots of battles are fought on this basis, in families and between nations.

You have beliefs. Many have been with you since before you could walk and talk – deeply cemented in the physical structure of your brain. Some you have picked up throughout life and some are surprisingly recent. Some are helpful, some are limiting.

The beliefs you hold about yourself shape the way you engage with life. So, what are they?

Bring no judgement to what comes up, simply notice what thoughts arise and immediately write them down. The time pressure helps you access your subconscious and grow your awareness of your hidden drivers.

Reflect & Write: Set a timer for 90 seconds and complete this sentence as many times as you can, 'I believe I...'

How's the balance of your list? What's the ratio of positive affirmations v negative perceptions of yourself? Let's attempt to balance it up, whatever you have fewer of, give yourself a further 90 seconds to add to them.

Beliefs can change. Your list is not cast in stone – you will not always believe these things about yourself. Let's prove it.

Reflect & Write: What three things did you once believe about yourself, that you no longer do?

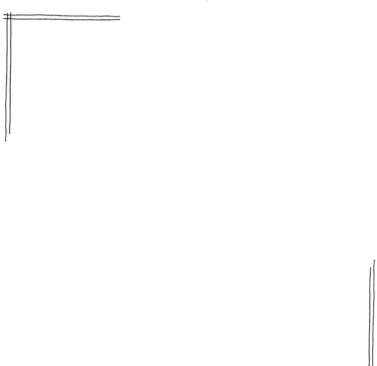

Here's a few of mine:
I used to believe I couldn't draw.
I used to believe results were all that mattered, not the process of getting them.
I used to believe chilling out was a waste of time.

If you accept beliefs can change, even the most entrenched ones, then you can become curious about what would happen if you could shift a limiting belief. Pick one from your list. It doesn't matter which one – remember, they're all beliefs not truths. Just put a line through it.

Reflect & Write: If you no longer held this limiting belief about yourself what difference would it make?

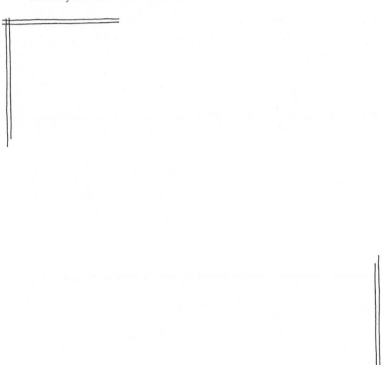

How does that feel? Maybe a little bit magical. Maybe unrealistic. Of course, shifting a belief isn't as simple as crossing the words out on a page. We'll look at how you grow later in the book. For now, though, all you need to know is that it is possible to change your beliefs. Just imagine at some point in the future, you're able to come back to the list of beliefs and genuinely strike off the limiting ones because you no longer believe them to be true.

Empowering, right!

OK. Just for fun, let's step into the shoes of the future version of you once again. This version of you is self-confident (without straying into arrogance). What positive beliefs does this version hold about you? Go for ten, in full sentences.

Reflect & Write: Complete this sentence ten times from the perspective of the future best version of yourself, 'I believe I...'

This future you sounds great, right? By now I'm hoping you want to be that person already. You have ten values, ten behaviours, and ten beliefs. Let's now add a set of skills.

CHAPTER 5
MY SKILLSET

What can you do?

Can you play an instrument, speak a second language or remember birthdays? Perhaps yes. I can't do any of these things. But I can cook a mean pizza, swim a mile, and publish books.

We all have a set of strengths that contribute to the positive state of our lives and a comparative set of weaknesses that may be more self-limiting. LinkedIn allows you to list 50 skills on your profile. So how many are there in total? Tonnes. And the vast majority of them I can't do: driving a fork lift truck, coding in C++, accounting. Let's not focus on what you can't do, we'll place your attention on what you *can* do, and what you'd like to learn how to do.

There's nothing fancy about this next question, so don't overthink it. Just make the threshold for writing it down really low – by this I mean, you don't have to be the best in the world at it in order for it to go on your list. For example, I'd write, 'I can draw' even though the reality in my household is that I'm third best at it (and perhaps my seven-year-old son will surpass my skill level one day too).

Reflect & Write: What can you do? Fill the page.

Have you included both soft skills and hard skills? If not, go back and add to the list.

'Hard skills' refers to technical knowledge or training that is specific to completing a task (e.g. website building, HGV license). 'Soft skills' are attributes that describe how you work individual or with others (e.g. teamworking, communication, creativity).

Now let's take a couple of different approaches to see if other skills emerge. As they do, add them to the list you already made.

Thinking of a successful project you completed, what did you do particularly well?

When working in teams what qualities do you bring?

When facing challenges, how did you overcome them?

In the past, people have said 'you're good at...'

Is your list growing? It should be. Now let's step out of thinking about yourself for a moment.

Reflect & Write: Think of five people you know personally who you admire in some way. Bring each to mind in turn and list their qualities (both their hard and soft skills).

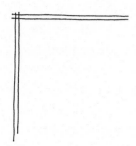

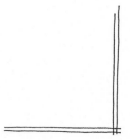

Was thinking about others easier or harder than thinking about your own strengths? Perhaps it felt less comfortable to consider your own qualities – and that may be because we can't see what we do well naturally, or because we've been socially conditioned not to boast and have zero practice at articulating what we're good at. We're changing that now. From the list of qualities of the people you admire, which ones could also relate to you? Add them to the list of skills you have.

You now have a long list of current skills, let's pare it back. Which are the five that define you best? Grab the word and then spend some time considering how this strength of yours plays a part in your life.

Reflect & Write: What five skills define you and how do you use them?

Now, let's consider the flipside of this coin, your weaknesses. By writing them down, their power to cause sleepless nights will dissipate, and by putting the impact into context, you can either let go of a problem that you thought you had, but don't, or make a decision to do something to reduce its impact.

Again, we'll start in a super simple way.

Reflect & Write: 'I am rubbish at…'. Just let the pen flow until no more come up.

How does that feel? There it is in black and white, on a single page – all the reasons why you beat yourself up. No matter how much development work you squeeze into your lifetime, you'll never empty this page. There will always be things you are not good at. So be OK with having a long list. Our goal together is not to eliminate it.

Instead, we'll immediately switch to a growth mindset. Stepping back into the shoes of your future best self, whose values, behaviours and beliefs you have already envisioned. What skills do they have? You already have the five banked from the earlier exercise, so now select five more.

Reflect & Write: Complete this sentence ten times from the perspective of the future best version of yourself, 'I am good at…'

This future you really is pretty awesome now.

CHAPTER 6
MY RECIPE

Reviewing everything you've noted down so far, consider each section to be an ingredient in the future best version of you: a handful of values, a sprinkle of behaviours, a bottle of belief, a dash of strengths, and a drop of weakness. You pour it all in, give it a stir and give it to a reporter to taste. This reporter then writes a paragraph or two.

Reflect & Write: Be the reporter, write about the character you're tasting.

You've just been writing about 'who am I' from a future perspective. But it's you, here in this moment, today, that has just done that. You have created this future version of yourself in your imagination.

It is still you. Authentically you. Just consciously shaped by you, rather than unconsciously moulded by other people. 'Your imagination is your preview of life's coming attractions', said Einstein. This is where your development journey is heading. In a moment we'll get back to the reality of where you're starting this journey from, today – but for now, just pause.

Read back what the reporter wrote about you. That's you they're talking about. Take a deep breath. Allow yourself to believe it could be the future you. Close your eyes and allow yourself to smile at the thought of it.

CHAPTER 7
SELF-ACCEPTANCE

The Myth of Okayness[2]

You may wish you were already different – or perhaps that others saw you differently. This is very common. In fact, in the top ten of 'How to...' Google searches in 2016 was 'How to accept myself for who I am.'

Sometimes we observe someone else and wish we were more like them. But remember, you're only seeing what they allow you to see. There is a whole hidden side that they keep private. When you ask, 'How are you?' and they respond, just like you do, 'Fine thanks', or 'OK', this the 'Myth of Okayness'.

If you really ask, and they really trust you, then you realize everyone has insecurities about who they are and a set of ways in which they would like to be different.

Consider people in the public eye who appeared to have everything and yet were or are fighting inner battles – Michael Jackson, Amy Winehouse, Princess Diana, George Michael, Tiger Woods, Marilyn Monroe. Who else would you add to this list? There will be many famous and successful people whose struggles have not yet made it into public awareness.

If it's OK for someone else not to be perfect, then it's OK for you to be imperfect too. A perfect human doesn't exist, can't exist, and therefore it isn't you and never will be. I'm not perfect and never will be, and neither will you. It's OK to be OK with not feeling OK about yourself, it's what makes us human.

Denial Is Futile

All of your past experiences have led you to this moment, and while you may not consider yourself to be flourishing, they lay the roots for your growth. You are you. Your past is in the past. Therefore, you have no option but to accept the embodiment of the you reading this sentence. You know what you've been through and how you have behaved; attempting to reject the past is futile. If you deny any thoughts or emotions, you'll be limiting your ability to grow and move beyond whatever is holding you back. Simply surrender to the peace that comes from acceptance. I am me, and for now, that is completely fine.

You Shape the You of the Future

Whilst you can accept that you are an embodiment of your past experiences right now, it isn't a done deal that you will remain this way forever. By choosing your future experiences, you'll be choosing to identify with new statements about yourself. As you'll see later, you can choose to let go of whatever 'I AM' statements you're holding onto right now that are not serving you well. How you grow is dependent on how you decide to nourish your roots.

Read this:

'I am imperfect and always will be. I accept that. I choose to release myself from self-judgement, and direct energy towards my growth.'

True. At least in spirit. Good. Let's channel the energy into why you are here.

CHAPTER 8
WHY I AM HERE

The Keel of Your Boat[3]

Imagine a flat-bottomed sailing boat. When the wind blows, the boat moves with it – and when the wind direction changes, the boat does too. And when there's a gust, pop, it capsizes.

To prevent this, boats have a keel that runs from front to back and cuts deep into the water. Now the boat moves in the direction it is pointing, (with the power of the wind captured by the sails) and stays upright while the storms blow strong.

A boat's keel is like your purpose in life. The more deeply connected you are with your sense of purpose, the more you're able to move in your chosen direction, achieving your dreams. The more deeply connected you are with your sense of purpose, the easier it is to stay upright when the winds of change blow and attempt to knock you off balance.

Does your life have a keel to keep you upright and pointing forwards? Is it there because of your social conditioning or because of your decisions?

Social Conditioned Purpose

We learnt earlier that social conditioning affects your sense of identity and shapes your purpose in life. From subtle unconscious bias related to the toys you were bought as a child, to 'help' from parents when choosing A-levels, and then degree courses; from social media influencers to the neighbours; what you are doing now has been influenced by the outside world.

When we're young, it's essential to listen to the advice of those people you trust to have your best interests at heart. At the right moments in life, it's important to recognize these influences AND ensure you're taking the ultimate decision about what you're choosing to do with your life.

Reflect & Write: Consider what you are doing now. Who influenced 'your' decision, and how have they influenced it?

What Is My Purpose?

First, we're going to soften the feel, by substituting the word 'purpose' with the word 'intention', and simply look at what intentions you have for your future and why they are important. For example, what is your intention for this weekend? (i.e. what do you intend to do?) There may be several things, so just choose one that is likely to be your highlight.

This weekend I intend to hang out with my daughter doing something we both enjoy. This is important to me because I feel as though, recently, we haven't spent quality time together, just the two of us. And that really matters to me because I want her to be able to talk to me openly as she enters her teenage years.

Reflect & Write: Now, over to you, complete this sentence: This weekend I intend to... this is important to me because... and that REALLY matters to ME because...

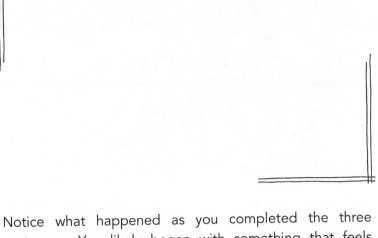

Notice what happened as you completed the three sentences. You likely began with something that feels superficial – a decision to do something out of habit, or because of some logical reason. As you moved through to the final sentence, you may have found that it feels a little more profound – coming from your heart rather than your head. It's this last sentence that gives you an idea about why you are doing it. It is your purpose. And therefore, you can now enquire if there is a better way of achieving the same purpose this weekend.

When you wrote the second sentence, did you find yourself struggling to find something to write? Perhaps what you intend for this weekend isn't important to you. Is there something else you would rather be doing with the most precious commodity of all, time?

There are plenty of weekends in life, so the stakes aren't that high really – it was just a practice round. Now let's expand the time horizon to six months.

Reflect & Write: What three intentions do you hold for yourself over the next six months? Follow the method from above, write down your intention, then why it is important to you, and finally, why that really matters. Complete this sequence for all three intentions.

Are you noticing a similar shift in your energy as you move through the series of questions? Allow the bottom sentences to be your keel.

Finally, we'll move the time horizon out to ten years. This is sufficient time for you to be doing pretty much anything you could imagine. Just let the pen flow, knowing that whatever emerges right this minute, is simply what emerges this minute and can be edited, replaced, or enhanced at any moment in the future.

Reflect & Write: What three intentions do you hold for yourself? Complete the sentence: In the next ten years, I intend to... And then follow the pattern from above: This is important to me because... And finally: This REALLY matters to ME because...

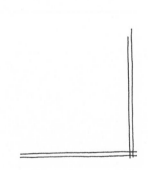

What you've written may have surprised you. Not many people spend focussed time considering the next ten years of their life; and if it's the first time for you, then be OK with your first draft of your future. You'll refine it, tweak it, tear it up – whatever. It's good enough to have a glimpse, however fleeting, of a deeper you.

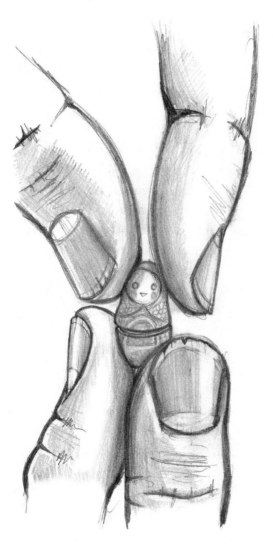

Bringing Intention to Life

It is possible to move through life without having a sense of purpose, and of course, it is possible to live a life without really having LIVED. By bringing intention to your future, you get connected to your keel. Here are some tips to help bring your intentions to life.

Tip 1: The Daily 3X

At the start of each day write down three things that will make this a great day (they have to be things within your control, so don't write something about the weather being nice!).

Tip 2: Annual Goals

What will make this a great year? Turn the intention into tangible milestones. If this year goes really well for you, what would you like to have achieved 365 days from now? Have a go now right now and then put monthly reminders in your calendar to check your progress.

Tip 3: Message in a Bottle

Have a guiding sentence that you can easily recall that helps you to make decisions. Will X or Y move me towards my life purpose? Know that this statement will evolve over time – but always have one.

Consider it this way: if you sat on a beach gazing out to sea and mulling over a significant life decision, what personalized message in a bottle would you like to wash up next to you which would help guide your decision?

Reflect & Write: What guiding message would you like to be reminded of every day? (Head to www.ownlife.me to be inspired by what others have written.)

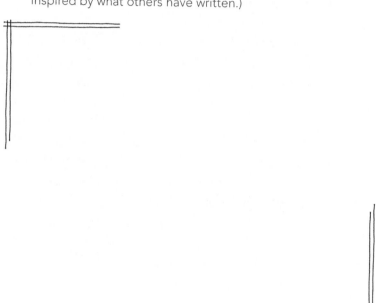

Getting Aligned

Consider what you are doing now. I don't mean reading this book. I mean in your life. Is it aligned with your sense of purpose? If yes, then great.

If not, then great! Often we can't stop doing what we're doing immediately without there being short-term consequences. However, the long-term consequence of continuing to do something that isn't aligned with your sense of purpose is more catastrophic. So simply noticing there's a gap is great. Being able to articulate that gap with some precision is even better as it's the first step to closing it. And greatest of all – is to write it all down so you can refer to it as we progress through the book.

Reflect & Write: When comparing what you're doing in life now against your long-term intentions, write down what thoughts arise.

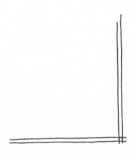

Concluding Thoughts

Using the exercises so far in the book, you now have a deeper awareness of the imperfect, unique human being shaped by all the experiences of your past. You painted a rich picture of the best version of you that could exist. And you've even taken a glimpse at what's even deeper inside – your purpose in life.

Your connection with a sense of purpose is so powerful, there's a whole book dedicated to helping you find it and achieve it. Take a look at *Own Life with Purpose*, it helps you to engineer a lifestyle that fulfils your dreams.

Who you are is a product of where you've been, but who you become is determined by where you go next. In part three of Own Life with Confidence we'll begin the journey towards becoming your best self.

PART 2

HOW I GROW

CHAPTER 9
YOU'VE CHANGED!

By accepting who you are today based on your past experience, you can now take active steps to decide who you'd like to be in the future. You are now an adult and the responsibility for who you are lies with you.

Since adolescence you've changed, you've overcome challenges, you've become good at some things, and with effort, you can become good at everything you want to. In Part 2 we'll put a spotlight on your habits, improve willpower and demonstrate that it's effort rather than innate talent that holds the key to your future.

Emerging from the Cocoon

You've seen how social conditioning affects who you are – and how things like beliefs and values are shaped by the people around you. However, we quite naturally begin the process of self-actualization – emerging from the childhood cocoon to become our unique butterfly. During our teenage years, tensions between child and parent often come from the teenager spreading their wings, questioning some beliefs, and choosing their friends and their environment.

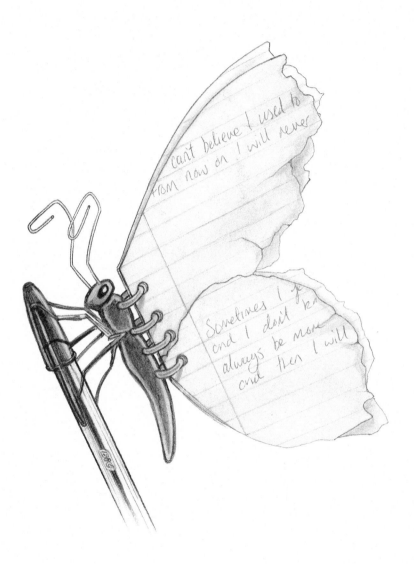

Reflect & Write: Reflecting on your teenage years, how did you emerge from the cocoon? Was it an easy transition, or were there tensions between you and your family? In what ways did you change? Write down ten changes that you are now noticing.

Reflect & Write: Looking back – what advice would you give to your 13-year-old self? Write a short paragraph.

Reflect & Write: How about the intervening years? In what ways have you changed since turning 20? Make a long list of skills, beliefs, environment, people you hang out with, what you do, what you wear, your hair, how you see yourself, and so on. Fill a page if you can.

When you look back, you'll notice there have been significant changes – some of it was deliberate and planned, but much of it simply happened. There's a lot changing that you're not even aware of from moment to moment. Did you know, for example, that 98 per cent of the atoms making up your body are replaced each year?[4]

Or when we say, 'it's in our blood', meaning something handed down through the generations, in fact, red blood cells only live for about four months?[5]

If you've ever believed that 'people can't change', it simply isn't true. You, me, and everyone else changes every day. Our daily experiences affect the synaptic connections in our brains. Change isn't only possible, it's inevitable.

Hermit crabs with too-small shells can't grow as fast as those with well-fitting shells and are likely to be eaten if

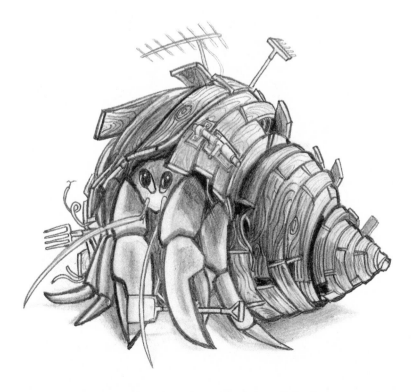

they can't retract completely. For us to Own Life, we must understand when we need to create more space to grow and be proactive about it rather than allowing the environment to squash us into our shell.

Back to the hermit crab for a moment – before moving into its new home, it must first choose to leave its snug environment, full of memories, and courageously scuttle into an expanse of no man's land where it is at its most vulnerable.

And so too, must we. The process of self-actualisation is not always comfortable, and at times, we have to summon real courage to leave our past behind.

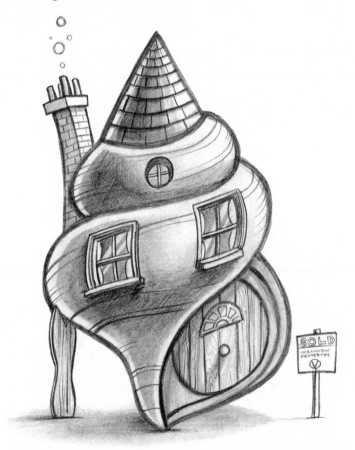

CHAPTER 10
SELF-ACTUALISATION

Overcoming Challenges

Whomever you are today, whether you are intensely self-critical, or coolly self-confident, there is an even better version of you waiting to emerge from beneath the layers of social conditioning. It is possible to bring 'conscious' change at many levels: in your environment, behaviour, capabilities, beliefs, values, or identity. It may seem hard now, but you've got some useful past experiences to draw from. It may seem daunting to leave the comfort of the past and take the first vulnerable 'crab-steps' into your future, so first let's look at how you've succeeded in getting to this moment in your life.

Reflect & Write: Consider the challenges from your past (e.g. moving schools, preparing for exams, delivering a speech, parents separating, finding a job, etc.), jot them down, aiming for ten or more.

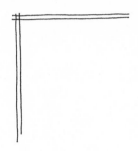

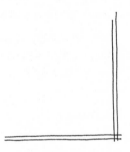

Focussing on the most difficult one, in the beginning, how were you feeling? Now you're reflecting on having successfully come through it, how do you feel? How did you do it?

Now back to the other nine on your list. What are you noticing? Maybe there's a pattern to how you overcome challenges. Maybe you're able to adapt your strategy each time a different challenge emerges. Maybe you get lucky.

Reflect & Write: When challenges presented themselves in the past, I successfully navigated them by...

Life is full of challenges, and the ones in front of us will always seem more daunting than the ones behind us. Yet, once upon a time, those challenges too seemed insurmountable. But here you are, reflecting on the lessons they brought you. These enable you to face the future, and scuttle into the unknown.

Becoming More You

Throughout this book, you'll be identifying things you want to shift to become an even better version of your true self. This process is termed 'self-actualization' and was first introduced by Adrian Maslow as the pinnacle of his 'Hierarchy of Needs'. Here is a selection of the most important characteristics, from his book Motivation and Personality.[6]

Use the list to audit yourself – tick each statement that is true for you:

- Self-actualized people embrace the unknown and the ambiguous.
- They accept themselves, together with all their flaws.
- They prioritize and enjoy the journey, not just the destination.
- While they are inherently unconventional, they do not seek to shock or disturb.
- They are motivated by growth, not by the satisfaction of needs.
- Self-actualized people have a purpose.
- They are not troubled by the small things.
- Self-actualized people are grateful.
- They share deep relationships with a few but also feel identification and affection towards the entire human race.
- Self-actualized people are humble.

A tough list right. For me personally, I still need to put conscious effort into the development of some of those bullets. Bring no self-judgement to the number of statements you ticked – all growth begins with self-awareness, so whatever your 'tick-count' you now have greater self-awareness. We've touched on some of the points already, and by the time you've worked your way through the book, you'll have covered them all. By then you'll be happy to let your true inner self shine through regardless of social etiquette, or dress code.

CHAPTER 11
HABITS

The Subtle Power of Habit

Almost half of our behaviours are repeated daily. These are the hidden habits that underpin our existence, so if we want to Own Life, we have to own our habits.

Scientists say that habits emerge because the brain is always looking for energy-saving initiatives and habits mean the electronic pulses of the brain can follow well-trodden pathways.[7]

Once a pattern is established, the synaptic connections are strong, and the brain can take a break from decision-making. Even if you successfully interrupt the pattern, the habit is literally encoded in the brain, ready to return when you let your guard down.

Try this right now. Put your hands out in front of you and interlock the fingers; notice which thumb is on top. Now take them apart and put them back together with the other thumb on top. How does that feel? Weird, right? You've formed a habit of doing it one way, you have no idea when that habit started and didn't even realize you had it until you just noticed it. Some people have the same habit as you, while others have the exact opposite.

To change a habit feels weird and you naturally want to

return to what feels normal. But if you keep noticing, keep practising the new way, then over a relatively short period, the new way becomes the habit, and it would be strange to ever go back again.

Reflect & Write: Consider your day so far in real detail from the moment you awoke. What have you done on autopilot? Can you identify 10, 15, even 20 things you have done without questioning them?

Helpful and Unhelpful Habits

Some habits are simply part of our routine – they don't bring real benefits or really get in the way. We tie our left shoe before our right or brush the upper left teeth before the lower left. We pick up the same brand of ketchup and open the curtains. We're simply efficient – reserving brain 'thinking capacity' for when it's needed later in the day. However, many habits have a much more profound impact on our lives. Some you may consider positive, and some you'd consider having a negative impact.

Reflect & Write: Make a list of ten helpful and ten unhelpful habits you currently have.

How Habits Form

Researched by MIT, and simplified by Duhigg[8], the neurological loop at the core of every habit consists of three parts: cue, routine and reward.

The routine is the behaviour (for example, checking my phone the moment I wake up, and then browsing it for 20 minutes). This routine first formed to satisfy a need for something, it was initially rewarding, and may continue to satisfy a craving. (My phone-checking habit started when I first installed Facebook and got a glorious shower of self-esteem endorphins every time I got a like, or someone accepted or sent a friend request. I was craving acceptance, friendship, love, and feared rejection.)

The Cue starts the habit loop. Almost all cues fit into one of five categories: location, time, emotional state, other people, or immediately preceding action[9]. Working through the phone-checking example, it takes a little thought to isolate the real cue. It's not location because I do it wherever in the world I wake up. It isn't time because I do it regardless of what time my alarm is set for. I don't think it's my emotional state because it happens regardless of how I feel in the morning, (and although I haven't tested this, I imagine it would happen whomever I wake up next to). So, it must be the immediately preceding action – waking from sleep. Now I have an autopilot loop which my conscious brain is giving no attention or energy to: Cue – alarm goes off; routine – I browse my phone; reward – I feel accepted.

How to Interrupt Habits and Form New Ones

To interrupt habits, we need to analyse the loop, starting with the current routine. This is the easy bit. The next job is to pin down the reward from the routine. What 'need' is this routine satisfying? What is the benefit? It is often a little more complex than you first imagine. 'I eat doughnuts to satisfy a hunger pang' may not be the whole truth!

It may also be difficult if we've spent the past trying to deny that any benefits to the habit exist. Take smoking. The reason people smoke, despite knowing the harmful health impact of it, is because it genuinely satisfies some craving. Only if we can get really honest with ourselves about the benefit of an unhelpful habit, can we begin to overcome it.

Once we understand the 'need' that the routine is satisfying, it's possible to set up some experiments to check if a different routine would result in the same satisfying feeling. If smoking is about getting away from the computer screen for five minutes and having a chat about something other than work, then would another routine have the same (or better) desired outcome?

Next, isolate the cue. Whenever the craving is first felt, log where, when, who with, how you're feeling, and what just happened. Hopefully, you'll begin to see a pattern.

Finally, have a plan and write it down. (Here's my plan to get over the compulsive early-morning phone checking: buy an alarm clock; leave my phone charging in the kitchen. Once I'm showered and dressed, use the time it takes to make and drink a coffee to browse my phone.)

The next activity will walk you through the process step-by-step and help you to be a habit changer for real!

Reflect & Write: Taking your list of ten unhelpful habits, which one would you most like to change? Write it as a goal statement: My goal is to...

Reflect & Write: Consider when the goal is accomplished, and you've successfully removed the old routine from your life. What difference does this make to you? The impact is...

Reflect & Write: What is the benefit of your current routine? What 'need' does it (or did it used to) satisfy? The benefit is...

Reflect & Write: What alternative routine could you experiment with that may achieve the same benefit? My new routine could be...

Reflect & Write: What is the cue that triggers the current routine (where, when, who, emotional state, or preceding action)? My cue is...

Reflect & Write: Knowing the cue will arise again in the future, and the same need requires satisfying, what plan do you have for a new routine? I plan to...

Now it's time to put that plan into action. Make notes on the result of your experiment. If things don't go perfectly at first, how will you adapt the plan until you are successful?

That's one habit tackled; but remember, the synaptic connections for the old habit are strong, and you may find yourself falling backwards from time to time. This is normal. It takes perseverance to make the changes really, truly, stick. If you do find yourself falling back to the old pattern, simply accept it has happened and recheck your motivation for changing by reviewing what you wrote about the impact of being successful. If it still holds true, and you still have a strong desire to change, run through the steps once more but this time with the benefit of being a little bit wiser.

You have identified another nine unhelpful habits. But changing one is enough for now. Shifting a habit isn't easy. Once you have the most important one locked down, return to the habit-changing process and tackle bad habit number two. For now, just know which one it will be.

Reflect & Write: The second habit I want to change is.... and the impact if I'm successful is…

Enough thinking about the 'bad' stuff you do for a while. Let's flip the coin and take a look at the other side.

Reflect & Write: You already listed ten positive habits. Which new ones would you like to add? Make a list of five, and then select the one that feels the easiest to achieve.

Reflect & Write: Write a precise goal sentence and the reason it's important to you: I would like to (the new routine)... because (the benefit it brings)...

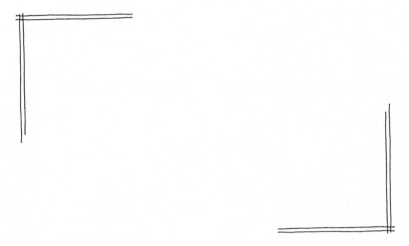

Reflect & Write: Now get really precise about the trigger for you to put the new habit into action. What is the cue? (Remembering: when, where, who, emotional state, preceding event). My cue is...

Reflect & Write: Write a list of all the things that could possibly prevent it from happening. What can you do to mitigate each one of them? How can you prepare for the moment in advance?

Keep a diary of your progress. Did you do it? If not, what got in the way and what have you learnt? If yes, how do you feel about it? Once you have the easiest one sorted and it happens on autopilot (i.e. it takes no conscious effort to make it happen), then move to the next easiest.

CHAPTER 12
SELF-CONTROL

Based on years of psychological research, Baumeister & Tierney[10] identified two traits that consistently predict 'positive life outcomes': intelligence and self-control.

Resisting the Marshmallow

When you listed all the things that could get in the way of successfully adopting the new habit, some will be external to you, and some will be internal. Did you have 'lack of willpower' on your list? It's perhaps the most common one.

In the early 1960s at Stanford University's Bing Nursery School, psychologist Walter Mischel gave children a choice between one reward (like a marshmallow, pretzel, or mint) they could eat immediately and a larger reward (two marshmallows) for which they would have to wait, alone, for up to 20 minutes. Years later, Mischel and his team followed up with the Bing pre-schoolers and found that children who had waited for the second marshmallow generally fared better in life.

Marshmallows might not be the thing you find difficult to resist. I've heard others say things like: coffee, beer/wine, TV binges, late nights, pressing snooze, checking emails at weekends, procrastination, and buying domain names.

Reflect & Write: What about you? List five areas where you believe greater willpower would be useful for you.

What Is Willpower?

Willpower is the ability to delay immediate gratification for the sake of positive future benefits. It has profound long-term consequences for health and wellbeing, and EVERYONE wants more of it!

The emotional brain is predisposed to exaggerate the value of immediate rewards and to severely discount the value of delayed rewards. The consequence is a natural over-prioritization of the short term over the long term, and a willpower challenge.

Having willpower strategies enables you able to balance the value of the rewards. You're able to push away short-term temptation in space and time (removing its immediate reward-giving powers), and bring distant rewards closer (both literally and metaphorically). Those that have established these strategies as habits could be labelled as 'having willpower', while those that don't employ the strategies may self-declare, 'I am impulsive'.

Reflect & Write: Mark an 'x' on the line and write down the reasons why you place yourself there.

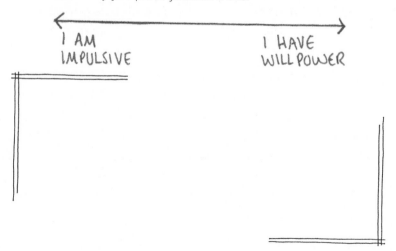

I AM
IMPULSIVE

I HAVE
WILL POWER

Like a muscle, willpower becomes fatigued with overuse, but it can be strengthened through training. Willpower isn't genetic and the strategies employed to develop greater self-control can be learnt. You can grow your willpower, and the following tips can help.

Strengthening Your Willpower Muscle

Tip 1 might surprise you. There is a direct correlation between glucose levels and willpower[11], when we're hungry, not only are we likely to be grumpy, we have less control over thoughts, emotions, impulse and focus. So eat! Properly! Sugar could bring a helpful short-term boost of willpower, but leads to sugar-crash and potentially, longer-term health problems. Go for foods with a low glycaemic index (GI) since the body converts them into glucose more slowly, and therefore produces a more sustainable performance level – think protein, vegetables, raw fruit, and nuts.

Tip 2 is equally underwhelmingly basic, (which could be either disappointing or pleasing to you). When you're tired, sleep!

Tip 3 takes us back to your simple daily habits. By trying to make a change to something super-simple, you begin to give the willpower muscle a daily workout.

Tip 4 relates to knowing we only have a limited supply of willpower, (it gets depleted throughout the day and recharged overnight), so the smartest strategy is to reduce how much you need by removing temptation. Instead of salivating and using the force of will to resist the marshmallow while staring at it, the kids that showed the best long-term results were those that turned away from it and did something completely different to distract themselves, effectively taking the tempting marshmallow out of the room. The people who believe they have strong willpower, are actually those who exert it least often (and therefore have it in reserve for when it's really needed). So, distance yourself from temptations that deplete your willpower reservoir.

Exercising willpower in one aspect of life has the wonderful natural consequence of greater willpower in other aspects without apparently trying. For example, working hard to stick to a gym routine may also be rewarded with less impulsive spending, greater focus at work and a tidier home.

Let's experiment with this hypothesis. Consider a task you always complete with your dominant hand – for example, using a spoon or brushing your teeth. Now use your other hand instead. Or try something more difficult; notice your speech patterns and how you insert 'filler' words or sounds, like 'erm', 'you know', 'like', and then begin to moderate your talking speed so you can eliminate them.

Reflect & Write: What will you try? Write it down, and then give it a go.

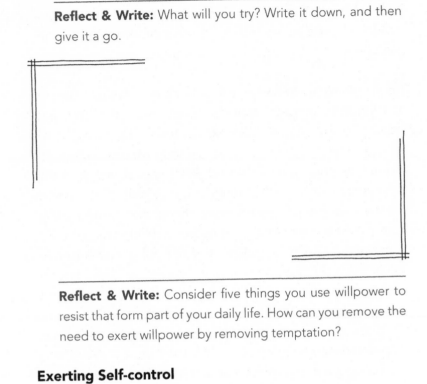

Reflect & Write: Consider five things you use willpower to resist that form part of your daily life. How can you remove the need to exert willpower by removing temptation?

Exerting Self-control

Reflect & Write: Now let's bring a specific topic into sharp focus. If you could bring self-control to a single aspect of your life, what would it be?

Reflect & Write: My self-control focus is...

Reflect & Write: Now let's set a realistic but stretching goal for it. Making sure that there is a timeframe attached to it: My goal is to...

Reflect & Write: What is the benefit of achieving this goal? Consider the long term and the short term: The benefit to my life is... The benefit to me every week of my life is...

Reflect & Write: Next, make a plan. Exactly how will you approach achieving this goal? I plan to...

When will you review your progress? Write down your review date. When the date arrives, note down EVERYTHING you have done that has broken the old habit, and be proud of having done it. Next, consider the gap between your actual behaviour and the original plan. What have you learnt?

It's unlikely that you've completely smashed it on one hit, but you've learnt a bunch of things you didn't know when you set the original plan, which puts you in a better place to make a better plan.

Reflect & Write: Complete this sentence: Based on my lessons, my new and improved plan is to...

CHAPTER 13
GROWTH MINDSET

Stripping back the work of Stanford University psychologist Carol Dweck into its most fundamental essence: A shift from 'I can't', to 'I can't yet' opens up a world of possibilities.

Fixed vs Growth Mindsets

All scientific 'laws' are actually hypotheses waiting to be disproved. And so is most of life, but we tend to believe things are more fixed than they are. Until they change. And the same is true for you.

One of the most basic beliefs we carry about ourselves has to do with how we view and inhabit what we consider to be our personality. In Carol Dweck's book, *Mindset*[12], she defines a 'Fixed Mindset' as one that 'assumes that our character, intelligence, and creative ability are static givens, which we can't change in any meaningful way'. Any success that comes is a reinforcement of the natural talents we are born with, rather than the result of striving. Individuals with a fixed mindset seek and repeat those activities that have a high probability of success (since it reinforces 'smartness'), and the prospect of failure is avoided at all cost (since it would indicate an insurmountable flaw in character).

A 'growth mindset', on the other hand, thrives on

challenge and sees failure not as evidence of an inbuilt deficiency but as an opportunity for growth. Those with a growth mindset believe they can get smarter, more creative, and more talented by putting in time and effort.

Since our early years, we have a bias towards one mindset or the other, which impacts our relationship to failure and, ultimately, our capacity for happiness.

Which Are You?

How many of the following statements can you respond to by wholeheartedly saying 'yes, that's soooo me'? Tick or cross them:

- I go after my dreams.
- I strive for progress, not perfection.
- Learning is my superpower.
- I am brave enough to try.
- I ask for help when I need it.
- I always strive to do my best.
- I seek new and difficult challenges.
- When I fail, I try again.
- I am a problem-solver.
- I stick with things and don't give up easily.

If your page is full of ticks, you're more likely to have a growth mindset. More crosses suggest that you currently tend to have a fixed mindset. Somewhere in between means there's plenty still to work on!

I Can't

Let's acknowledge there are a whole bunch of things you can't do. I'll start you off with a list that jumps into my head within ten seconds:

I can't speak French, run a marathon, stop craving coffee, grow younger, remember names, move to another country, afford to take six months off to travel the world, live my kids' lives for them, remember to floss every day, engage well on social media, fix a particularly bad relationship, or shoot straight on Fortnite.

Reflect & Write: Go on, I've shared mine, your turn. What's on your list? Write down at least ten.

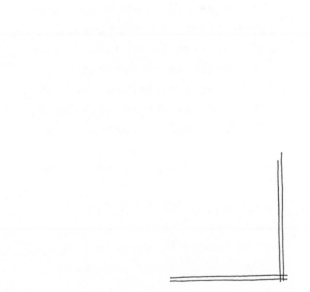

I Can't... Yet

Did your parents ever say to you 'There's no such thing as "can't",' Well, without the benefit of Carol Dweck's research budget, they were hitting the nail on the head. As simple as

je ne peux parler français

it sounds, and despite the waves it is making in the world of education, a growth mindset boils down to putting a single word at the end of a very common sentence – I can't... yet.

Go back to your list above and write 'yet' at the end of every statement. There will be some that don't make sense so cross those ones off (I genuinely can't grow younger). There may be items on your list that would be undesirable even if you could do them, so they can go too (I really shouldn't want to live my kids' live for them). There may be some on your list that is low priority (I can't speak French, but I don't feel it's holding me back).

What remains is the important stuff, and with the word 'yet' added, it can feel quite liberating. I can learn to play the guitar, I can develop the capacity to speak in public, I can beat my craving, I can learn to remember names.

I simply haven't executed the right strategies, or found the right teacher, or made it a priority, or persevered when things were difficult. All of which can be fixed.

Experimenting with a Growth Mindset

After learning the theory, I put it into practice. First, I visited a primary school in East London and was shown paintings the class had mad using photos of themselves dressed up as kings and queens to copy from. I saw what I'd expect to see – faces, crowns, gowns – the primary elements of the photos. But, not stopping there, the class adopted a growth mindset.

They gave themselves some feedback – what three things did they notice that were different between their painting and the original photo. Then they took feedback from their teacher, and finally from a six-year-old classmate. They had a second attempt at the painting. Then there was a second round of feedback and a third attempt at the painting. The whole process took only two weeks, and yet if you'd asked me to guess the ages of the children who painted the third pictures, I'd have said they were many years older.

Applying the process I learnt from six-year-olds, I challenged the story that I'd been telling myself for decades, the one that said, 'I can't draw.' For the first time ever, I had a real go at drawing something to the best of my abilities. I drew my son – and here is my first attempt. I was quite proud of it and could have stopped there.

But I'd visited the six-year-olds, so I applied the growth mindset, received feedback in a grateful way, believed I could improve, and gave it a second attempt. Again, I was pleased with the outcome and impressed with the progress I had made. And could have stopped. But I'd seen the evidence of the impact of a third attempt at the primary school. After another round of feedback, a week later I drew this picture of my daughter.

For 41 years, I believed I couldn't draw because I wasn't born with a talent. Now I know I can draw, and it wasn't talent that I'd previously lacked, it was self-belief and effort.

The process only took three weeks and I'm now more open to challenging my other long-held negative self-perceptions too. Over the next few pages, we'll be helping you to bring a growth mindset to your current limiting beliefs.

Effort Over Talent

The '10,000 hours of practice' concept can be traced back to a 1993 research paper written by Anders Ericsson[13] and made popular in Malcolm Gladwell's book *Outliers*[14]. Ericsson's findings, which are not universally agreed on, were that individuals who have a talent for a specific discipline were overtaken by individuals with less natural talent but a better attitude towards practice. Even further – anyone could become a world expert at anything if they practice diligently for 10,000 hours, regardless of initial talent.

While we could spend energy trying to unpick the research methodology, it points to a common phrase that's often forgotten, 'practice makes perfect' (which I'd prefer to adapt to 'practice makes progress'). Without needing to read research papers, we can all agree that the more time we invest practising something, the better we get.

Earlier you listed the things you can do and for me this included making awesome pizzas. I can now look back and reflect on my learning journey from complete incompetence through to where I am now, and it would look something like this:

- Buy supermarket frozen pizzas (10 years)
- Buy ready-made pizza bases, a jar of pizza sauce, and add my own toppings (5 years)
- Buy *River Cottage Veg Everyday* cookbook and follow the pizza dough recipe to the letter with varying degrees of success (5 times)
- Learn by experimenting to hone the cookbook recipe to my personal preference (30 iterations) – for example, pre-cooking the base for 5 mins to firm it up then wrapping it in tea towels which keep the moisture in and prevent it being overly crisp
- Get lucky by using a different sauce ingredient (when my regular one was out of stock) and finding it makes the flavour POP!
- Every time I make pizza, keep our family favourites but always experiment with a new topping variant (15 times)

Was I born a talented pizza maker? No. I applied a growth mindset and acquired the skill.

Reflect & Write: Go back to your list of what you can do well and analyse how you become good at it. Do it for five different strengths.

Your notes now contain the strategies you've employed to achieve mastery. They may include perseverance, a great teacher, openness to feedback, self-awareness, acceptance that failure is part of the learning process, dedication, focus, prioritization, resilience, taking one step at a time, desire.

For some of your strengths, you remain on a steep learning curve – so keep doing what you're doing. For others, your level of expertise may have begun to 'flatline' – you're no longer improving and may be resting on your laurels. It's a strength that could become a super-strength if you chose to reapply the growth mindset to it.

Reflect & Write: Choose one from the list that has a high number yet has 'flatlined'. Imagine you could be the best in the world at that thing (or simply the best person that you know of). What do you intend to do now to restart the process of mastery?

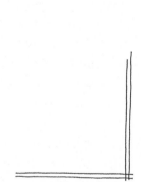

Start with a Single Step

You've just been thinking about how to get better at something that you're already good at; to keep raising the bar. For everything on that list, you started off as a complete novice. Your long journey to mastery started with a single (probably) wobbly step.

Reflect & Write: Go back to your list of 'I can't' statements. Choose one that you'd really be proud to be able to say 'I can' to and one that would make a difference to your professional life. Start your sentence with 'I can't...' and end it with '... yet.'

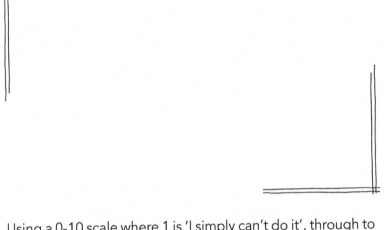

Using a 0-10 scale where 1 is 'I simply can't do it', through to a 10 which is 'world mastery', then a 4 would be something like 'I'm not quite OK at it'. You may achieve a single ten in your lifetime, and the items in the box above are likely to score between 0 and 4. If it's holding you back then it needs to be addressed, if you are to *Own Life with Confidence*.

How will you begin? It's unlikely to be with a giant four-point leap from one to five. It's more likely to take micro-steps of confidence-building. Ask yourself: What would cause me to feel slightly more confident at this thing? This becomes your very first action. So, when will you start? What does success look like at a 2? Don't look beyond and define your goal based on being a 7 – start by being realistic. Only when you've reached a 2, ask yourself what could cause me to feel slightly more confident? What does success look like at a 3? And what baby step will I take next?

By the way, success at step 1 is simply to have given something a go. Bring no judgement to the outcome – you've broken a habit of not trying anything, and you deserve a medal simply for giving it a go. Regardless of the external result, you are growing internally.

Reflect & Write: Write down the very first baby step you plan to experiment with for both your 'I can't... yet' statements from the previous box.

When you take this step, you move closer to being better at something that's important to you. Congratulations! Now plan the next baby step.

Remember, you can become good at virtually anything – it just takes self-belief and perseverance.

PART 3

GROWING INTO THE BEST
VERSION OF ME

CHAPTER 14
THE BEST VERSION OF ME

This is where we pull the strands of everything we've done together into a single red thread that flows through the book in your hand and out into the remainder of your life. Part 1 established acceptance of the authentic person you are today, and Part 2 introduced the tools and mindsets required to be deliberate about your growth.

Quite nicely, on our journey through 'who am I', we occasionally paused to imagine the best version of you that is ready to emerge. You therefore have everything you need to create your growth map: the starting point; the destination; and the compass. In this final part you'll plot your path.

Is it that simple? Are you thinking 'the future best version of me seems so different to the me that defined it'? That may be true. I hope it's true. The best version of you should be aspirational, something dreamy, almost unbelievably good. Let's not set our sights any lower. And then let's not judge the 'you' of today by the mythical standards of the 'you' of the future. No. The only helpful judgement for today is: Am I applying a growth mindset?

There's a rule of thumb in aviation, a one degree change in direction leads to a one-kilometre change in destination for every 60km flown. In other words, if a small change is applied consistently over a long enough period of time then the results can be huge. It's by applying this philosophy that you'll incrementally, almost unnoticeably at first, begin to metamorphose into the person you have visualised.

There're some beautiful consequences to this methodology:

- it's low risk because each small step feels safe
- because we're building habits, the 1 degree becomes locked on autopilot and becomes effortless
- as we take the journey we can update the destination and make tiny adjustments to trajectory in order to get there

Each and every action you take or word you speak contributes to the future life you will live. You're about to create your own future by making one-degree tweaks to what you do every day. Does that sound like a good investment of your energy? Sure it does!

OK, let's pick up the work from Part 1 and refresh the aspirational version of you that is ready to emerge. But I don't want you to turn back to your earlier notes and simply create a summary – nor do I want you to go back to the words you wrote when you were standing in the shoes of the reporter. If we did that, it would be your brain doing the work and it's likely you'd end up with a precise list of things that make up the future you, but without emotions attached to it. We'll introduce a different technique here, one that taps into a deeper level of authenticity.

You are going to write. Your pen hits the paper and for a whole ten minutes it does not leave the page. When you are pausing to think about what to write next, leave the pen touching the page. Your task is simply to give your hand complete freedom to transcribe all the thoughts that arrive in your mind in full sentences. Unfiltered. Unedited. Unjudged. Unstructured. Just write and write and write. Later you'll be the editor. Not now. Now you are simply a writer.

The work you did in Part 1 is on paper in this book – it's also been in your subconscious mind, maturing nicely. You'll access this depth of insight by following the instructions to simply be the writer. So let's go for it.

Reflect & Write: Set a timer for ten minutes and simply write. Start with the following words, and then just let the pen flow: The best version of me…

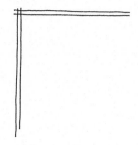

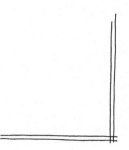

How was that? Is your hand aching? You perhaps haven't written that much by hand since sitting in school exam halls! Many people report being surprised by what they've written, or how easily the pen flowed – it couldn't go fast enough to keep up with the outpouring of thoughts – or that the ten minutes flew by.

Now let's add anything that's missing from your fast writing session. Check back to everything you wrote in Part 1, are there some skills, values, behaviours or beliefs which would enhance this vision of the best version of you? Go back and add to your notes above.

That's it. Contained in those scribbles is you, ready to be revealed to the world as soon as we've gently removed the outer layers of social conditioning.

Next we allow the role of the editor to say hello. You may believe in the law of attraction which is based on the idea that positive or negative thoughts bring positive or negative experiences into a person's life. I like to simplify it: you get what you focus on. This is why we spend time visualising the future version of you, writing down what we see and using multiple lenses to look at the same thing. My wish for you is that your editor will produce a succinct articulation of the best version of you, which is easily referenced in your mind and felt in your heart on a regular basis. In ever decreasing numbers of words, you'll be capturing the essence of every tiny detail you want to incorporate in the future you.

Put the pen in the hand of the editor inside you. Go back to your quickly written scribbles – underline, star, cross out, circle – mark up your notes to pick out the highlights.

Reflect & Write: Taking your annotated scribbles, write two paragraphs in full sentences and with correct punctuation that contain the essence of the most important things from your notes.

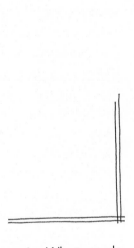

Sit back from the page, re-read it. And again. What words do you want to change to tighten it up, or alter to make it more authentically you? Do you need to insert an adjective to lift its aspiration?

Done? Keep reworking it until it is. There's no need to rush – precise words are important. This is the story you'll be telling yourself over and over, so it's helpful, important, essential even to make sure the story is written well.

Reflect & Write: Imagine being that person. It is going to happen. How do you feel? Capture it in one sentence.

Look at the words you just wrote. Feel the sensation in your body as you read them. Notice your posture. Where is your energy? Those words are your magical motivators. Look for somewhere to write them so you see them every day and allow them to seep into your subconscious.

CHAPTER 15
THE ONE DEGREE MAP

You already know the present version of you, the one reading this sentence, the one who has sufficient growth mindset to choose to invest in their own personal development. Taking the mindset that you get what you focus on, we're going to place our attention on the one percent improvements you can make, rather than assassinate the current imperfect version of you.

You will shortly turn the future version of yourself into a list of ten 'more' statements. They are 'more' because we want the future version of you to be more you! If you start with a 'less' statement, then flip the wording so it is positively framed. Let me give you some examples.

The future me is more:

- Relaxed and able to enjoy each passing moment fully
- Sociable and enjoys conversations over dinner with friends
- Gentle with my expectations of others
- Impactful across the world through my writing and videos

- Financially independent from corporate clients
- Supportive of the most vulnerable people in society
- Trusting of people to support my most important goals
- Present in my parents' lives
- Willing to spend money on one-off experiences
- Skilled at film making

You see that none of them place judgement of a lack of something now, even though all of them could have been written with a negative frame, e.g., stop hoarding my money for the future. With this orientation I can be OK with the me of today, and smile at the better version that will emerge. So now over to you.

Reflect & Write: Starting from the you of today, what more is required in order for you to become the best version of you in the future? (List the ten most impactful things).

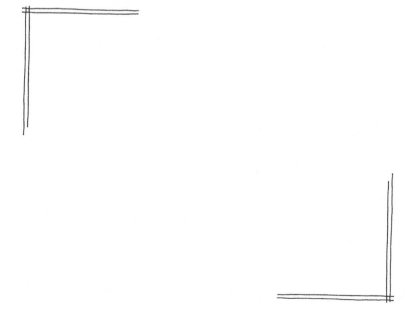

Remember back to the impact of a one-degree shift in trajectory now, and how such a small change can lead to big results if it is sustained over a long enough period of time. For each of the things on your 'more' list, what's the one degree of change you can implement in your life now?

Here's mine, related to my previous list:

1. Take my espresso and drink it outside in the garden instead of whilst I'm working
2. When meeting a neighbour, be ready to give the conversation as much time as it needs rather than trying to exit it quickly
3. I'm struggling with this one. The problem is that others see me set high standards for myself and feel they need to match it – I'm not willing to lower my personal standard and I'm not sure what the right words could be that wouldn't feel condescending to say, 'I don't expect as much from you!'. I'll need to sleep on this one.
4. Finish this book and then re-watch the 'Advertising for Authors' course
5. Even when busy with corporate work, reserve 20% of my working hours for personal projects
6. Pursue my Samaritans application
7. Give trust to my wife to make family decisions independently
8. Fortnightly Zoom calls on Sundays as a routine
9. Follow up the Hot Tub hire we did in January, by hiring or booking something for the family to experience in August
10. Set aside two hours per week to learn about film directing

Reflect & Write: For each 'more' statement, what's the one-degree change you are able to make in your life now?

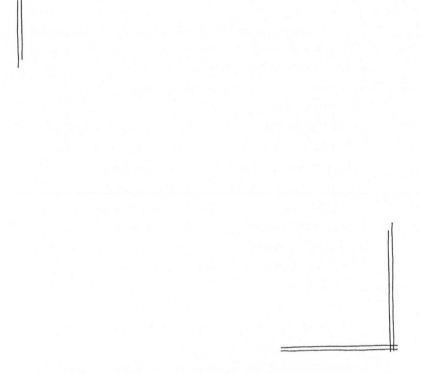

If I do the things on my list then I will have adjusted my course by one degree and every day I will become closer to the best version of me that I've envisioned. The same is true for you. Once I've cemented a behaviour in my lifestyle, I can contemplate stretching things a little further, for example, not just taking my espresso outside during a break but taking a walk with my wife at lunchtimes. But that's for later, for now, we only need to focus on the first step.

In Part 2 we acknowledged that change isn't as simple as writing a list. You have ingrained habits, willpower deficiencies and fixed mindsets to overcome. But you didn't just notice these difficulties, you grew in your awareness of how to overcome them and in many cases already have small experiments planned to give yourself confidence in your ability to make change stick.

To finish the route map, we're going to put the two elements together: the change you want and the change toolkit. Here's how it will work.

Take your first 'future me' goal (mine is to be relaxed and able to enjoy each passing moment fully), put this into the first box on the next page. Then use the questions that follow to guide your application of the change toolkit. There's a double page spread for each of your ten 'future me' goals. Here's the set of questions you'll be exploring with some guidance on each:

1. The future me is more...
Copy the words you wrote previously – e.g. relaxed and able to enjoy each passing moment fully

2. The one-degree change I will implement now is...
Copy the words from the last Reflect & Write section – e.g. take my espresso and drink it outside in the garden instead of whilst I'm working

3. Design the habit loop (cue, routine, reward)
Be microscopic in the details you put into your routine, entirely unambiguous about the cue, and pause to imagine how you will feel rewarded for successfully doing it. Working through my example:
Cue: I pick up my hot espresso

Routine: I walk to the back door unlock it, slip on my shoes, walk down to the bench at the top of the garden, place my cup on table, sit down, take a breath, hear a bird sing, take my first sip. After taking the last sip, take a breath, hear a bird sing, return to the house and continue with my day. (If it's raining then I take a seat by the window and look outside).

Reward: A feeling of calmness as I return to my desk

4. How can I give willpower a helping hand?

Remember that old habits are deeply ingrained in the brain and therefore take less brain energy than your new planned behaviour, also that your brain is predisposed to value immediate benefits over delayed ones. My autopilot would grab the coffee and return immediately to work, grateful it has barely cost me a minute of working time. Now I'm asking my brain to override the default pattern and give up the reward of getting things done for at least five minutes. This takes willpower, so what can you do to give willpower a helping hand?

In my example it's about eliminating any excuse that my subconscious could make about it taking longer than it needs to. So, in advance, I prepare the coffee machine, make sure the keys are by the door, as are my shoes and coat. I have thought about looking up a way to lock myself out of my computer for five minutes, but this feels extreme (for now anyway). I also considered putting a timer on my phone so that I didn't speed drink the coffee and return too quickly, but I'd rather not have my phone with me. So for now, I'm going to experiment with just making the path to the garden bench as free from obstacles as possible.

5. Growth mindset check

This is how you measure yourself as you begin applying the experiment. You're not judging the outcome, as there are many variables that can affect this – a poorly designed experiment (what to do when I'm not working from home), some external interference (such as my wife seeing me drinking a coffee and joining me for a chat), some assumption that wasn't correct (birds would be singing). No, what you're judging is the attitude you're bringing to the experiment. We're defining attitude as 'a growth mindset' which includes: acceptance that mastering a task takes effort rather than talent; you apply grit and determination; you regard failure as an opportunity to learn rather than evidence of inability.

Decide how frequently you want to measure your mindset, date each line, and complete it when the date rolls around.

6. Constant improvement

Each time you pause to score your mindset ask yourself, what have I learnt that will improve the likelihood of this change sticking? If everything is working perfectly then just write this and keep doing it. If there is even the tiniest tweak to make, then write this into your habit loop or willpower helping hand box. If the experiment needs a full rewrite, then do this. Go back to box two and write a new one-degree change you plan to try.

7. Change secure. Next step.

You only get to write in this box when you have full confidence your one-degree change is embedded in your autopilot. When this is true for you, reading your box one, what is the next one-degree change you are ready to implement that will take you closer towards the 'more you' goal?

1. The future me is more…

2. The one-degree change I will implement now is…

3. Design the habit loop (cue, routine, reward)

4. How can I give willpower a helping hand?

5. Growth mindset check

Date:

1 2 3 4 5 6 7 8 9 10

1 2 3 4 5 6 7 8 9 10

1 2 3 4 5 6 7 8 9 10

1 2 3 4 5 6 7 8 9 10

1 2 3 4 5 6 7 8 9 10

6. Constant improvement

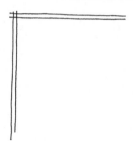

7. Change Secure. Next Step

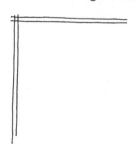

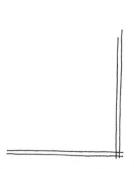

1. The future me is more…

2. The one-degree change I will implement now is…

3. Design the habit loop (cue, routine, reward)

4. How can I give willpower a helping hand?

5. Growth mindset check

Date:

1 2 3 4 5 6 7 8 9 10

1 2 3 4 5 6 7 8 9 10

1 2 3 4 5 6 7 8 9 10

1 2 3 4 5 6 7 8 9 10

1 2 3 4 5 6 7 8 9 10

6. Constant improvement

7. Change Secure. Next Step

1. The future me is more…

2. The one-degree change I will implement now is…

3. Design the habit loop (cue, routine, reward)

4. How can I give willpower a helping hand?

5. Growth mindset check

Date:

1 2 3 4 5 6 7 8 9 10

1 2 3 4 5 6 7 8 9 10

1 2 3 4 5 6 7 8 9 10

1 2 3 4 5 6 7 8 9 10

1 2 3 4 5 6 7 8 9 10

6. Constant improvement

7. Change Secure. Next Step

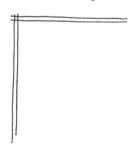

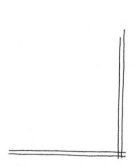

1. The future me is more…

2. The one-degree change I will implement now is…

3. Design the habit loop (cue, routine, reward)

4. How can I give willpower a helping hand?

5. Growth mindset check

Date:

1	2	3	4	5	6	7	8	9	10
1	2	3	4	5	6	7	8	9	10
1	2	3	4	5	6	7	8	9	10
1	2	3	4	5	6	7	8	9	10
1	2	3	4	5	6	7	8	9	10

6. Constant improvement

7. Change Secure. Next Step

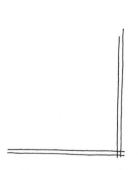

1. The future me is more…

2. The one-degree change I will implement now is…

3. Design the habit loop (cue, routine, reward)

4. How can I give willpower a helping hand?

5. Growth mindset check

Date:

    1 2 3 4 5 6 7 8 9 10

    1 2 3 4 5 6 7 8 9 10

    1 2 3 4 5 6 7 8 9 10

    1 2 3 4 5 6 7 8 9 10

    1 2 3 4 5 6 7 8 9 10

6. Constant improvement

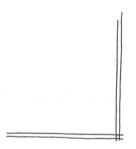

7. Change Secure. Next Step

1. The future me is more…

2. The one-degree change I will implement now is…

3. Design the habit loop (cue, routine, reward)

4. How can I give willpower a helping hand?

5. Growth mindset check

Date:

| 1 | 2 | 3 | 4 | 5 | 6 | 7 | 8 | 9 | 10 |

| 1 | 2 | 3 | 4 | 5 | 6 | 7 | 8 | 9 | 10 |

| 1 | 2 | 3 | 4 | 5 | 6 | 7 | 8 | 9 | 10 |

| 1 | 2 | 3 | 4 | 5 | 6 | 7 | 8 | 9 | 10 |

| 1 | 2 | 3 | 4 | 5 | 6 | 7 | 8 | 9 | 10 |

6. Constant improvement

7. Change Secure. Next Step

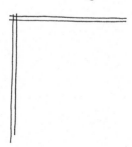

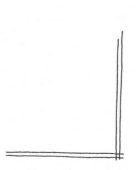

1. The future me is more...

2. The one-degree change I will implement now is...

3. Design the habit loop (cue, routine, reward)

4. How can I give willpower a helping hand?

5. Growth mindset check

Date:

1   2   3   4   5   6   7   8   9 10

1   2   3   4   5   6   7   8   9 10

1   2   3   4   5   6   7   8   9 10

1   2   3   4   5   6   7   8   9 10

1   2   3   4   5   6   7   8   9 10

6. Constant improvement

7. Change Secure. Next Step

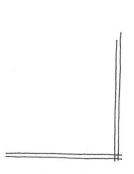

1. The future me is more…

2. The one-degree change I will implement now is…

3. Design the habit loop (cue, routine, reward)

4. How can I give willpower a helping hand?

5. Growth mindset check

Date:

	1	2	3	4	5	6	7	8	9	10
	1	2	3	4	5	6	7	8	9	10
	1	2	3	4	5	6	7	8	9	10
	1	2	3	4	5	6	7	8	9	10
	1	2	3	4	5	6	7	8	9	10

6. Constant improvement

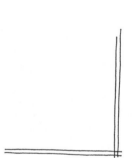

7. Change Secure. Next Step

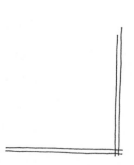

1. The future me is more...

2. The one-degree change I will implement now is...

3. Design the habit loop (cue, routine, reward)

4. How can I give willpower a helping hand?

5. Growth mindset check

Date:

1 2 3 4 5 6 7 8 9 10

1 2 3 4 5 6 7 8 9 10

1 2 3 4 5 6 7 8 9 10

1 2 3 4 5 6 7 8 9 10

1 2 3 4 5 6 7 8 9 10

6. Constant improvement

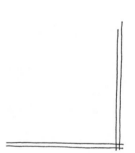

7. Change Secure. Next Step

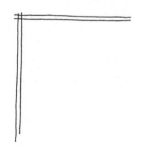

1. The future me is more...

2. The one-degree change I will implement now is...

3. Design the habit loop (cue, routine, reward)

4. How can I give willpower a helping hand?

5. Growth mindset check

Date:

1 2 3 4 5 6 7 8 9 10

1 2 3 4 5 6 7 8 9 10

1 2 3 4 5 6 7 8 9 10

1 2 3 4 5 6 7 8 9 10

1 2 3 4 5 6 7 8 9 10

6. Constant improvement

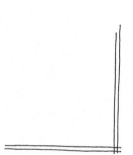

7. Change Secure. Next Step

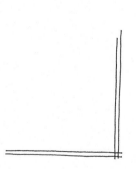

EPILOGUE –
OWN ALL OF LIFE

Change is inevitable, but who is driving it? You truly can choose what an enhanced version of yourself looks like and you really can develop the skill of self-control. It takes effort to change, and you'll hit difficulties. But you've already shown remarkable resilience and an ability to overcome challenges. The evidence is that you're here, investing time in your personal growth.

When I try to imagine that I can one day master something that I'm currently incompetent at (like speaking French), it can feel like an impossible dream. It can feel daunting. Yet one small step leads to another and the daunting limits simply dissolve as I approach them.

You don't need to know how you will take the final step, the answer to that will emerge when you take the one before it. All you need to do is start walking.

From this day forward, change your internal story from 'I'm no good at…', to 'I'm bringing a growth mindset to get better at…'. I believe you are capable of doing this. The evidence is that you're here, at the back of the book, still reading. So keep it up and over time you'll begin to believe in yourself, too.

How's It All Going?

I asked you this question right at the start of the book. Let's pause again to step back from the details of life, and check in. Well done for choosing to invest some time in yourself and pat yourself on the back for persevering to the end of the book – many of the self-reflection questions I posed are quite challenging.

Reflect & Write: Having worked through *OWN LIFE WITH CONFIDENCE* I will...

If you're ready to continue your OWN LIFE journey, where do you want to focus next?

OWN LIFE WITH COURAGE: How to thrive on the emotional rollercoaster of life

OWN LIFE WITH PURPOSE: How to engineer a lifestyle that fulfils your dreams

OWN LIFE WITH TRUST: How to develop positive relationships

Congratulations on choosing to develop yourself. If this becomes a lifelong habit I guarantee you a wonderful life and I wish you the very best of luck with it.

DEAR READER...

The very best thing about what I do is when I get to see people grow into their own skin and radiate a comfortable ease that only comes with being their wonderful authentic self. The magic is multiplied when I get to be a witness (and occasional mentor) as they continue their life journey. I would love to add you to the community of people I know who are actively working on improving themselves.

From time-to-time I share stories of my journey. The successes and the struggles. I also test new material and ask for guidance from my readers on what would be most helpful in the future. If you'd like to be a part of the Own Life community go to www.ownlife.me/connect

And... you can make a big difference to me right away.

Reviews are the most powerful way for an independent publisher like myself to help new readers find my books. And reviews are the most trusted source when new readers are choosing how to spend their money.

Honest reviews of my books help to nourish the entire system. If you've enjoyed this book, I would be super-appreciative if you could spend just five minutes leaving a review (which can be as brief as you like).

I really hope that I've been able to help you on your Own Life journey.

With big thanks,

todd@ownlife.me

ABOUT THE AUTHOR

Todd Eden's sole mission in life is to bring out the best in people. It wasn't always this way! Right through childhood and through his first couple of careers, he was insatiably competitive – great at bringing out his personal best and achieving results, but not always with great consideration for everyone around him.

Thankfully he married someone who simply oozes kindness. The resulting upgrade, Todd version 2.0, retains his authentic ambition to win at life but now defines winning as 'bringing out the best in others'.

This mission has taken him around the world working with multi-national companies; into the lecture theatres of a third of the UK's universities; and deep into the lives of his personal coaching clients.

He remains a passionate student of self-development and has been living and breathing it daily for decades. At live events he enjoys bringing his unique combination of profound life shifting moments with belly laugh humour to thousands of people. It's his wish that this book brings out the best in many thousands more.

Connect with Todd at www.ownlife.me/connect

ABOUT THE ILLUSTRATOR

From a young age, El Davo enjoyed art, and from seeing other people's reactions, he learned he had a talent. He attributes some of this to being curious and observational of his surroundings – or a daydreamer as others might put it. Those around him saw the need to nurture this talent well before he was aware of it himself.

He was lucky enough that his older sister was an artist, always there to offer invaluable support and encouragement when he was growing up. She lived in London at the time and regularly took him around the city to different galleries, as well as showing him all the graffiti and street art hotspots. Later she convinced him to pursue an art education beyond sixth form and attend art college, and after that, university.

Initially, he never felt like he'd earned this talent, but nonetheless felt obliged to make the most of it. He constantly strives to improve, for both the buzz of exceeding his own expectations and the joy it brings others. He especially loves to hear of people inspired enough to get back into doing art themselves. He firmly believes there's a huge pool of untapped creative talent in society, stuck inside people who haven't had the support and encouragement he's been fortunate enough to receive.

Connect with El Davo at www.eldavo.co.uk or on Instagram @eldavooo

"I believe in myself. I know and accept myself for exactly who I am today and feel inspired by how I will grow into the future."

[You, 6 months from now]

How to Grow Into the Best Version of Yourself

Accept yourself for who you are today, with all the beautiful flaws, without judgement

Clearly see a future enhanced version of yourself that is still authentically you

Overcome resistance to change and keep the development journey rolling

"My inner world is a positive place even when the outside world has its ups and downs. I'm resilient to setbacks and have found courage to push through fears that used to hold me back."

[You, 6 months from now]

How to Thrive on the Emotional Rollercoaster of Life

Create a separation between external events and internal emotions

Reprogram the filters through which you experience the world

Dare to do what you dream by pushing through fear

"I know where I'm heading in life and am grounded enough to enjoy each passing moment. I dream big, set plans, and make them happen. It's a thrill to be alive."

[You, 6 months from now]

How to Engineer a Lifestyle that Fulfills your Dreams

Turn dreams, wishes and hopes into goals that feel tinglingly possible

Give focus to your most precious priorities as you become a blackbelt time master

Feel alive every day with energy habits that boost resilience

"From making a good first impression to repairing age-old broken relationships; from deepening my most loving friendships to navigating conflict, I build trust with others."

[You, 6 months from now]

How to Develop Positive Relationships

Reframe your attitude to conflict through an enhanced desire to see new perspectives

Respond with calm maturity when triggered by the behaviour of others

Unleash the simple magic of listening with wholehearted attenti

ENDNOTES

1 Eagleman, D. (2016) The Brain, The Story of You. Edinburgh: Canongate Books. Page 6

2 First heard from Nigel Linacre (NigelLinacre.com)

3 Metaphor conceived by Jefferson Cann (JeffersonCann.com)

4 Opfer, C. (2014) 'Does your body really replace itself every seven years?' 6 June 2014. HowStuffWorks.com. <https://science.howstuffworks.com/life/cellular-microscopic/does-body-really-replace-seven-years.htm>

5 Radford, B. (2011) Does the Human Body Really Replace Itself Every 7 Years. 4 April 2011. LiveScience.com. <https://www.livescience.com/33179-does-human-body-replace-cells-seven-years.html>

6 Maslow, A. (1997) Motivation and Personality. Pearson

7 Duhigg, C. (2013) The Power of Habit. London: Random House Books.

8 Duhigg, C. (2013) The Power of Habit. London: Random House Books

9 Duhigg, C. (2013) The Power of Habit. London: Random House Books. Page 283

10 Baumeister, R & Tierney, J. (2012) Willpower. London: Penguin Books. Page 1

11 Baumeister, R & Tierney, J. (2012) Willpower. London: Penguin Books. Page 50..

12 Dweck, C. (2012) Mindset. London: Robinson.

13 Ericsson, K., Krampe, R., and Tesch-Romer, C. (1993) The Role of Deliberate Practice in the Acquisition of Expert Performance. Psychological Review, vol. 100. No3, 363-406

14 Gladwell, M. (2009) Outliers: The Story of Success. London: Penguin

INDEX